# Creative Alchemy

## Unleashing Generative AI's Artistic Potential

# Creative Alchemy

## Unleashing Generative AI's Artistic Potential

**Digvijay Kumar Tiwari**

Bigfoot Publications

*Because, there's a writer in everyone.*

Bigfoot Publications
*Because, there's a writer in everyone.*

**Creative Alchemy: Unleashing Generative AI's Artistic Potential**
**Author :  Digvijay Kumar Tiwari**

**First Published by**
Bigfoot06 Publications (OPC) Pvt. Ltd.
B-10,12 Shree Shyam Palace,
Sector 4,5 Chowk, Old Railway Road,
Gurugram, Haryana (122001)
Website: www.bigfootpublications.in
Email: info@bigfootpublications.in

**First Edition : September,  2023**
© **Digvijay Kumar Tiwari**

ISBN Print Book - **978-81-19512-60-7**



Printed in India

# TABLE OF CONTENTS

# INTRODUCTION

In the age-old pursuit of creativity, humans have harnessed their imagination to create works of art, music, literature, and design that transcend time and culture. But what happens when we infuse the power of artificial intelligence into this creative equation? The result is a remarkable fusion of human ingenuity and machine learning, a phenomenon we explore in depth in this book, "Creative Alchemy: Unleashing Generative AI's Artistic Potential."

From the first flicker of cave paintings to the grandeur of Renaissance masterpieces, the trajectory of human creativity has been intertwined with technological advancements. Today, we stand at the precipice of another artistic revolution—one that's not limited to human hands and minds alone. Generative AI, an exciting offshoot of artificial intelligence, has proven itself to be more than a tool; it's a collaborator, an inspiration, and a provocateur of novel ideas.

As we venture into the pages of "Creative Alchemy: Unleashing Generative AI's Artistic Potential" we're embarking on a journey that transcends the boundaries of traditional creative realms. Generative AI, driven by advanced algorithms and neural networks, is capable of producing art that speaks to the soul, music that evokes emotions, and literature that sparks imagination. This isn't mere imitation; it's a creative process that challenges our perceptions of authorship and creativity itself.

This book is your guide to understanding the intricate workings of Generative AI and its transformative impact on artistic expression. We'll peel back the layers of neural networks, delve into the nuances of Generative Adversarial Networks (GANs), and unravel the algorithms that are breathing life into AI-generated content. But beyond the technicalities, we'll explore the heart of creativity—the very essence that makes art a universal language.

Through the chapters ahead, you'll witness how AI can summon visuals that range from the surreal to the sublime, compose symphonies that resonate with the human spirit, and even draft narratives that captivate the mind. But this isn't just a showcase of AI's capabilities; it's an exploration of the connections between human creators and their digital counterparts. It's a celebration of the symbiotic relationship between imagination and computation.

Yet, our journey is not without its ethical crossroads. We'll confront the biases that can permeate AI-generated content, and we'll ponder the implications of a world where machines actively contribute to the creative landscape. We'll address the concerns of authenticity, the potential displacement of artistic roles, and the delicate balance between human guidance and AI autonomy.

"Creative Alchemy: Unleashing Generative AI's Artistic Potential" is an invitation to contemplate the redefinition of creativity as we know it. It's an opportunity to witness the evolution of artistry, to grasp the potential of AI to amplify human visions and to navigate the uncharted waters of innovation and responsibility. Whether you're an artist seeking new mediums, a technologist fascinated by AI's artistic prowess, or a curious soul eager to understand the future of creativity, this book is your compass through the vast landscape of Generative AI.

So, let's embark on this journey together—a journey where pixels, notes, and words become the palette of a new artistic era. Prepare to witness the fusion of human dreams and computational prowess, and to unveil the secrets of "Creative Alchemy: Unleashing Generative AI's Artistic Potential" that can unleash Generative AI's unparalleled artistic potential.

# CHAPTER 1
# FOUNDATIONS OF GENERATIVE AI

In the ever-evolving landscape of artificial intelligence (AI), the concept of generative AI stands as a testament to the remarkable strides made in creative machine learning.

At its core, generative AI represents a paradigm shift, enabling machines not only to process and analyze data but to actively create entirely new content. This foundational aspect of generative AI serves as a bridge between data-driven insights and imaginative innovation, ushering in a new era of possibilities across industries.

To comprehend the intricacies of generative AI, it is imperative to first grasp the broader landscape of AI, machine learning, and deep learning. AI, the overarching field, encompasses the creation of intelligent systems that can perform tasks typically requiring human intelligence.

Machine learning, a subset of AI, empowers computers to learn patterns and make decisions from data, while deep learning employs neural networks with multiple layers to achieve advanced feats of recognition and prediction. Within this framework, generative AI emerges as a distinct branch, dedicated to enabling machines to autonomously generate content, thereby transcending mere pattern recognition to artistic creation.

Generative models form the crux of this field, exemplified by their ability to generate new data that adheres to the underlying patterns of the input data. Among these models, Generative Adversarial Networks (GANs) and Variational Autoencoders (VAEs) stand as prominent examples. GANs introduce a revolutionary approach through a two-agent system: a generator creates data, and a discriminator evaluates it. This adversarial interplay results in the refinement of the generator's capabilities, ultimately yielding novel content that often baffles the line between human and machine creation. On the other hand, VAEs adopt an encoder-decoder structure to map input data into a latent space and reconstruct it, permitting the generation of similar yet unique data points. This ability to traverse latent spaces and create entirely new variations unveils the latent potential of generative AI.

Throughout history, generative AI has witnessed remarkable milestones that have shaped its trajectory. From early attempts at image synthesis to the advent of GANs and their transformative impact on generating hyper-realistic images, the journey of generative AI is a testament to the relentless pursuit of creativity within machines. As we embark on a journey to understand the foundations of generative AI, we delve into the intricate interplay of data, models, and algorithms that empower machines to transcend their conventional roles and join humanity on the path of imaginative exploration.

## Understanding machine learning and neural networks

In the landscape of modern technology, machine learning stands as a monumental leap in the realm of artificial intelligence. At its core, machine learning is a paradigm through which computers gain the ability to learn from data without explicit programming. This revolutionary approach empowers machines to recognize patterns, make informed decisions, and improve their performance over time, mirroring the way humans learn from experience. At the heart of machine learning's success lies the concept of neural networks, intricate systems that simulate the interconnected web of neurons in the human brain.

Neural networks serve as the foundation upon which many machine learning models are built, and they play a pivotal role in enabling computers to perform complex tasks such as image recognition, language translation, and even creative generation. These networks consist of layers of interconnected nodes, or artificial neurons, each designed to process and transform input data. The connections between these neurons carry weights, representing the strength of the relationship between them. During training, these weights are adjusted through a process known as backpropagation, where the network fine-tunes its internal configurations to minimize errors between predicted and actual outcomes.

Deep learning, a subset of machine learning, has surged to prominence in recent years due to its remarkable ability to process and analyze vast amounts of complex data. Deep learning models, often referred to as deep neural networks, are characterized by their depth—the numerous layers of neurons they contain. This depth allows them to capture intricate hierarchies of features in data, making them exceptionally adept at tasks such as image and speech recognition. Convolutional Neural Networks (CNNs) specialize in processing grid-like data, like images, by applying filters that detect specific features, while Recurrent Neural Networks (RNNs) are tailored for sequential data like text, speech, and time-series data.

The advent of neural networks has unlocked possibilities previously considered in science fiction. For instance, the concept of transfer learning involves training a neural network on one task and then adapting it to perform a different but related task. This approach has fueled the development of pre-trained models that can be fine-tuned for specific applications, greatly accelerating the pace of innovation.

As we navigate this landscape, understanding neural networks is pivotal to comprehending the potential and limitations of modern AI. The elegant yet intricate structure of these networks, inspired by the biological neurons of the human brain, has revolutionized our ability to process information, learn from data, and emulate cognitive functions. With each advancement in machine learning and neural networks, we take a step closer to bridging the gap between human and artificial intelligence, unlocking the potential for machines to learn, adapt, and contribute in ways previously unimagined.

## Differentiating between supervised, unsupervised, and reinforcement learning

Machine learning, the backbone of modern AI, encompasses a spectrum of methodologies, each tailored to specific tasks and objectives. Among the cornerstones of machine learning are three distinct paradigms: supervised learning, unsupervised learning, and reinforcement learning. Understanding the nuances and applications of these paradigms is essential for navigating the multifaceted landscape of AI.

**Supervised Learning: Guided Intelligence**

Supervised learning serves as a trusted guide for AI models in their quest to learn patterns from data. This paradigm thrives on labeled examples—datasets where each data point is accompanied by the desired outcome. The process unfolds as an AI algorithm analyzes the input data and its corresponding outcomes, learning to map inputs to outputs accurately. It's akin to teaching an AI system by showing it explicit examples of what's right. Supervised learning finds its foothold in tasks like image classification, where an algorithm learns to classify images into predefined categories based on labeled training data. This paradigm is like a mentor that trains the AI to recognize the world as it's been defined.

**Unsupervised Learning: The Quest for Hidden Patterns**

Unsupervised learning, on the other hand, delves into the mysteries of uncharted data without predefined labels. In this paradigm, the AI seeks to uncover inherent structures or relationships present in the data itself. Unsupervised learning doesn't come with a predetermined guide—it's an explorer wandering through the data's landscape, deciphering patterns on its own. Clustering and dimensionality reduction are typical applications of unsupervised learning. Imagine an AI sifting through customer purchasing data to uncover segments or groups that emerge naturally, revealing valuable insights into customer behavior without any explicit instructions.

## Reinforcement Learning: Learning through Interaction

Reinforcement learning is the agent of exploration, a paradigm that learns from interaction with its environment. In this scenario, the AI agent takes actions to maximize a cumulative reward over time. It navigates the environment, receives feedback in the form of rewards or penalties, and adjusts its actions accordingly. It's the realm of trial and error, where AI systems learn through repeated experiences. A classic example is training an AI to play a game—through repeated attempts, it learns to take actions that lead to higher scores. Reinforcement learning is akin to teaching a pet new tricks; it thrives on experimentation, adaptation, and a quest for optimal strategies.

## Synthesis of Learning Paradigms: A Holistic Approach

While these paradigms may seem distinct, they often synergize to create sophisticated AI systems. Semi-supervised learning combines elements of both supervised and unsupervised learning, leveraging labeled data alongside unlabeled data to improve performance. Transfer learning involves training models on one task and transferring the learned knowledge to another, which often incorporates elements of both reinforcement and supervised learning. These paradigms aren't isolated islands—they're threads interwoven into the fabric of AI's capabilities.

In understanding the intricacies of supervised, unsupervised, and reinforcement learning, we gain a compass to navigate the spectrum of AI's potential. These paradigms, with their distinct approaches and applications, equip us to address a diverse array of challenges, unlocking AI's capacity to learn, adapt, and contribute across a myriad of domains.

**Explaining the basics of generative models: autoencoders, variational autoencoders, and generative adversarial networks (GANs)**

Generative AI is the realm of machines that possess the remarkable ability to create content that mimics the patterns and structures present in the data they've been trained on. At the core of this transformative field lie generative models—algorithms designed to capture the essence of data distributions and synthesize new content that adheres to these patterns. Among the pioneers of generative models are autoencoders, variational autoencoders, and the groundbreaking generative adversarial networks (GANs).

**Autoencoders: Unveiling Hidden Representations**

Autoencoders are akin to magicians performing an act of data compression and reconstruction. Imagine a neural network that compresses a large image into a compact code and then reconstructs the image from that code. Autoencoders consist of an encoder, which compresses the input data into a lower-dimensional representation, and a decoder, which attempts to recreate the original input from this compressed code. The beauty lies in the hidden representation—latent space—formed in the middle. Autoencoders learn to capture the most important features of the input data in this latent space, effectively distilling complex information into a compact form.

**Variational Autoencoders (VAEs): Navigating the Latent Continuum**

Variational autoencoders (VAEs) build upon the autoencoder concept, adding a touch of probabilistic elegance. In VAEs, the latent space is not a single point but a distribution—a range of potential values. This distribution enables VAEs to generate new content that adheres to the learned patterns. VAEs are not just about compression and reconstruction; they are about generating new content that is often a synthesis of multiple points in the latent space. VAEs excel at creating new data points that fit within the boundaries of what they've learned, offering a peek into the realm of creativity.

## Generative Adversarial Networks (GANs): The Creative Duel

Generative adversarial networks (GANs) are the trailblazers that shook the foundations of Generative AI. Imagine two artists—a counterfeiter and an art critic—engaged in a creative duel. The counterfeiter, known as the generator, crafts artwork, while the art critic, or the discriminator, scrutinizes it. This adversarial interplay fosters a process where the generator continuously strives to create content that's indistinguishable from real data, and the discriminator aims to tell the difference. This cat-and-mouse game drives GANs to create content that's astonishingly realistic. GANs have the potential to generate images, music, text, and more that can often blur the line between human-created and AI-generated.

## A Holistic Perspective:

While these models have their unique attributes, they collectively breathe life into the concept of Generative AI. Autoencoders lay the foundation for understanding latent representations, VAEs introduce a probabilistic twist to creativity, and GANs exemplify how competition can foster innovation. Together, they form the spectrum of generative models, each contributing its unique hue to the canvas of AI-generated content.

In unraveling the basics of these generative models—autoencoders, VAEs, and GANs—we peer into the mechanisms that AI employs to conjure art, music, and more. These models serve as the toolkit for machines to capture patterns, traverse latent spaces, and engage in creative duels, revolutionizing the landscape of human creativity and innovation.

## Real-world applications of Generative AI: image generation, text generation, music composition, and more

The impact of Generative AI transcends the confines of research labs, seeping into the very fabric of our daily lives. From the stroke of a virtual brush to the composition of melodious tunes and the crafting of engaging narratives, the real-world applications of Generative AI are as diverse as they are transformative.

### Image Generation: Where Pixels Paint Dreams

Generative AI has wielded its virtual brush to create stunning visual art, blurring the line between human creation and machine ingenuity. These algorithms can generate landscapes that enthrall, portraits that captivate, and abstract compositions that challenge our perception. Applications range from assisting artists in conceptualizing ideas to enhancing virtual environments and aiding architects in envisioning spaces. With Generative AI, pixels have become the paint, and algorithms the artists—collaborating to produce art that both mesmerizes and inspires.

## Text Generation: Penning Words Beyond Imagination

In the realm of literature and communication, Generative AI has become a wordsmith of unparalleled prowess. Whether conjuring up poems, penning news articles, or even crafting fictional stories, AI-generated text is a testament to its capacity to understand language and context. Chatbots driven by Generative AI can hold conversations that mimic human interactions, revolutionizing customer service and personalized communication. These algorithms have even delved into the world of content creation, producing written material that's informative, engaging, and in some instances, virtually indistinguishable from human-written text.

## Music Composition: The Symphony of Binary Notes

The ethereal world of music has also succumbed to the allure of Generative AI. These algorithms can compose melodies that span genres, evoke emotions, and explore harmonies that human composers might not have considered. Music generated by AI has been featured in video games, movies, and even live performances, showcasing the adaptability of Generative AI in contributing to the auditory landscape. By learning the patterns of existing compositions, Generative AI offers a fresh perspective on musical creation, presenting compositions that traverse the realms of the familiar and the innovative.

## Fashion Design: Threads of Artificial Couture

In the world of fashion, Generative AI has woven threads of innovation, contributing to the creation of unique designs and patterns. These algorithms can analyze existing styles, trends, and fabrics to create new clothing designs that merge tradition with modernity. Fashion designers and brands are leveraging AI to explore new frontiers of creativity, with AI-generated designs gracing runways and collections. This fusion of human creativity and machine-generated aesthetics has redefined how we envision the future of fashion.

## Scientific Discovery and Drug Design: Unlocking New Frontiers

Beyond the realms of art and aesthetics, Generative AI has proven its mettle in scientific exploration. AI models have been employed to generate molecular structures with potential applications in drug design and materials science. These algorithms can predict molecular properties, identify potential compounds, and even contribute to accelerating the drug discovery process. The marriage of AI's computational power with the ingenuity of human scientists is revolutionizing research and innovation, potentially ushering in breakthroughs that address some of humanity's most pressing challenges.

In embracing these real-world applications, we witness Generative AI's evolution from a concept to a reality that touches multiple facets of our lives. From generating captivating visuals and thought-provoking text to composing harmonious melodies and aiding in scientific research, the capabilities of Generative AI are an ode to the union of human creativity and technological advancement.

# CHAPTER 2
# GENERATIVE ADVERSARIAL NETWORKS (GANS)

In the realm of Generative AI, few innovations have ignited as much excitement and fascination as Generative Adversarial Networks, or GANs. This chapter delves into the mesmerizing world of GANs, a groundbreaking concept that has redefined the landscape of content generation. GANs introduce a unique interplay of competition and collaboration, where two neural networks engage in a creative duel, pushing the boundaries of what machines can create. As we venture into the heart of GANs, we unravel the inner mechanics of their adversarial dance, explore their diverse applications, and ponder the profound implications of this dynamic approach to content creation. From lifelike images to imaginative text and beyond, GANs stand as a testament to the synergy between ingenuity and computation, painting a new paradigm for AI-generated creativity.

## Deep dive into GANs: generator and discriminator networks.

At the core of Generative Adversarial Networks (GANs) lies a captivating interplay between two neural networks—the generator and the discriminator. This dynamic duo constitutes the heart and soul of GANs, working in tandem to achieve an unparalleled level of creativity and realism in AI-generated content.

## The Generator: Crafting Imaginary Realities

The generator network is the creative force in the GAN ecosystem. Its role is akin to that of an artist or a composer, conjuring up content from nothingness. Given a seed of random noise as input, the generator uses its layers of interconnected nodes to transform this noise into something meaningful—whether it's an image, a piece of text, or a musical sequence. Through the training process, the generator learns to map the latent space of random noise to the space of real data. It's like teaching an artist to paint by showing them a vast array of images, allowing them to internalize the patterns and styles inherent in the data. With each iteration, the generator strives to create content that's increasingly indistinguishable from real data, blurring the line between human and machine creation.

## The Discriminator: The Connoisseur of Authenticity

The discriminator, on the other hand, plays the role of a discerning critic or an art detective. Its task is to differentiate between real data and the content produced by the generator. Essentially, the discriminator is trained to recognize the nuances and features that characterize genuine data. As it scrutinizes both the content produced by the generator and real data, it refines its ability to distinguish between the two. This adversarial process of training the discriminator involves providing it with labeled data to facilitate its learning. The discriminator's mastery lies in its capacity to scrutinize even the tiniest details, uncovering the subtle markers that denote authenticity. It becomes an art critic, skilled at detecting both the brilliance and the forgery in the gallery of generated content.

## The Dance of Adversarial Training: A Creative Tug-of-War

The magic of GANs unfolds through an iterative dance—a creative tug-of-war—between the generator and the discriminator. The generator strives to produce content that the discriminator cannot differentiate from real data, while the discriminator evolves to become more adept at telling the difference between the two. With each iteration, both networks refine their skills, leading to a convergence point where the generator becomes so adept at creating content that it can often deceive even the discriminator. This dynamic interaction results in content that exudes realism, mirroring the data patterns from which the GANs have learned.

As we plunge deeper into the workings of GANs, we unlock the essence of their creative prowess. The adversarial synergy between the generator and the discriminator transcends mere algorithms, delving into the realm of creativity itself. This duality of creation and discernment allows GANs to craft content that tantalizes the senses and challenges our perceptions of human and machine creativity.

**Training process and optimization.**

The training process of Generative Adversarial Networks (GANs) is a captivating dance of competition and collaboration a digital duel between the generator and the discriminator. This process is guided by optimization techniques that seek to fine-tune the networks, allowing them to reach a delicate equilibrium where the generator creates content that is almost indistinguishable from real data. Let's delve into the intricacies of the GAN training process and the optimization strategies that underpin this fascinating interplay.

**Adversarial Training: Iterative Refinement**

The training of GANs unfolds through a series of iterations, each consisting of a two-step process: one for the generator and another for the discriminator. In the generator step, random noise is input to the generator, which produces AI-generated content. This generated content is then fed into the discriminator, along with real data. The discriminator evaluates and assigns probabilities to the input data being real or generated. This feedback is sent back to the generator, enabling it to adjust its parameters to create content that's more convincing.

**Loss Functions: Guiding the Duel**

Loss functions are the North Star that guides the optimization process in GANs. For the discriminator, the loss function measures how well it distinguishes between real and generated data. The generator's loss function, on the other hand, gauges its ability to fool the discriminator. The tug-of-war between these loss functions steers the adversarial training—bringing the networks closer to achieving a balance where the generator creates content that's virtually indistinguishable from real data, and the discriminator struggles to differentiate between the two.

## Vanishing Gradient and Mode Collapse: Challenges to Overcome

The GAN training process is not without its challenges. One common issue is the vanishing gradient problem, where gradients become extremely small, hindering effective learning. Another challenge is mode collapse, where the generator focuses on producing a limited set of content that tricks the discriminator without displaying the diversity found in the training data. Researchers have developed strategies, such as modifying the loss functions or introducing regularization techniques, to mitigate these challenges and foster more stable training.

## Optimization Algorithms: Steering the Learning Process

The optimization algorithms used to train GANs are fundamental in navigating the complex landscape of parameter adjustments. Techniques like stochastic gradient descent (SGD) and its variants, such as Adam, are employed to iteratively update the network parameters based on the gradients calculated from the loss functions. Fine-tuning these optimization algorithms is crucial to ensure that the networks reach a state of equilibrium without one overpowering the other.

## Convergence and Challenges: Seeking Equilibrium

The ultimate goal of GAN training is to achieve convergence—an equilibrium where the generator produces content that is truly lifelike, and the discriminator's ability to differentiate between real and generated data becomes progressively challenging. Achieving this balance is an art that requires tweaking hyperparameters, adjusting loss functions, and experimenting with optimization strategies.

The training process and optimization in GANs are akin to orchestrating a symphony—an intricate interplay of variables and strategies to bring about a harmonious convergence of creative forces. As the generator and discriminator networks refine their skills through adversarial training and optimization, they pave the way for a new era of AI-generated content that challenges artistic norms and redefines our understanding of creativity.

## GAN variations: conditional GANs, styleGANs, and cycleGANs.

The landscape of Generative Adversarial Networks (GANs) is a tapestry woven with variations and innovations, each tailored to address unique challenges and unlock novel capabilities. Among the notable GAN variations are Conditional GANs, StyleGANs, and CycleGANs. These variations infuse GANs with added dimensions, enabling them to create content that's even more customized, expressive, and transformative.

## Conditional GANs: Customizing Creativity

Conditional GANs introduce a paradigm where both the generator and the discriminator receive additional information—known as conditions—in addition to the random noise. This information serves as a guideline, steering the content creation process in a specific direction. For example, in image generation, the conditions could be labels indicating the type of object to generate. This variation allows for highly tailored content creation, ensuring that the generated output adheres to the desired criteria. Conditional GANs have applications in various domains, including image-to-image translation, where they enable the creation of specific visual outputs based on input conditions.

## StyleGANs: The Artistry of Aesthetics

StyleGANs bring a new dimension of control to the GAN landscape, focusing on the artistic nuances of content generation. StyleGANs enable the disentanglement of content and style in the generated output. Content represents the core structure of the output, while style pertains to the finer details and aesthetic elements. This separation empowers creators to manipulate the style of the generated content, allowing for the synthesis of images with specific artistic traits. The versatility of StyleGANs is evident in applications like image synthesis and artistic manipulation, where they give rise to content that is not only realistic but also artistically expressive.

## CycleGANs: Bridging Domains and Realities

CycleGANs embark on a journey of domain adaptation and style transfer. These networks specialize in translating content from one domain to another while preserving essential characteristics. For instance, CycleGANs can transform images of horses into images of zebras or turn paintings into photographs while retaining the style and essence of the original. The distinctive feature of CycleGANs is their capacity to learn mappings between domains without requiring paired data for training. By employing cycle consistency loss, these GANs ensure that translating content back and forth between domains yields content that remains coherent and representative of the source and target domains.

## Unveiling New Horizons:

These GAN variations—Conditional GANs, StyleGANs, and CycleGANs—usher in a new era of versatility and specificity in AI-generated content. They extend the boundaries of creativity and innovation, enabling GANs to adapt to specific conditions, create content with artistic finesse, and seamlessly traverse between different domains. These variations not only showcase the dynamic nature of GAN research but also hint at the vast potential of Generative AI to reshape industries, art forms, and human-machine collaboration.

## Ethical considerations and challenges in GAN-generated content.

As Generative Adversarial Networks (GANs) continue to push the boundaries of AI-generated content, they also raise a host of ethical considerations and challenges that warrant careful contemplation. The transformative power of GANs in generating highly realistic and creative content comes with a responsibility to address these concerns and ensure that the impact of AI-generated content aligns with societal values.

## Misuse and Deception: The Dilemma of Authenticity

One of the key ethical concerns with GAN-generated content is its potential for misuse and deception. GANs have the capacity to create content that is nearly indistinguishable from real data, blurring the line between genuine and fabricated. This can give rise to the spread of fake news, misinformation, and deepfakes—audio or visual content that can be manipulated to deceive viewers. The challenge lies in devising mechanisms to authenticate and verify content to prevent the exploitation of GANs for malicious purposes.

## Privacy and Consent: The Ethical Quandary

GANs can synthesize images and content that closely resemble real individuals. This raises profound privacy concerns, particularly in scenarios where GANs are used to generate synthetic images of people without their consent. These images could be used for unauthorized purposes, infringing upon personal privacy and rights. Addressing these challenges requires stringent regulations and guidelines that safeguard individuals' privacy and consent in the context of AI-generated content.

## Bias and Fairness: Unintended Replication of Inequities

AI systems, including GANs, can inadvertently replicate biases present in the training data. If the training data contains biases related to race, gender, or other attributes, GANs may generate content that perpetuates these biases. The responsibility lies in curating diverse and representative training datasets and implementing techniques that mitigate bias, ensuring that AI-generated content does not amplify societal inequalities.

## Ownership and Intellectual Property: Navigating New Frontiers

The question of intellectual property ownership in the realm of AI-generated content is a gray area. If GANs produce content that mirrors existing copyrighted material, who holds the rights? Does the creator of the GAN, the owner of the training data, or the GAN-generated content itself claim ownership? Clarifying these legal and ethical complexities is crucial to fostering a fair and just environment for content creation and distribution.

## Transparency and Attribution: The Need for Accountability

As AI-generated content becomes more integrated into various domains, the issue of transparency and attribution gains prominence. Should AI-generated content be labeled as such? Should consumers be aware when they interact with content generated by machines? Striking a balance between transparency and seamless integration is essential to foster trust and ensure that users can make informed decisions.

## The Path Forward: Responsible AI Creation

Navigating the ethical considerations and challenges associated with GAN-generated content requires a multifaceted approach. Collaboration among researchers, policymakers, ethicists, and industries is crucial to developing robust guidelines, regulations, and technologies that promote responsible AI creation. Ensuring transparency, fairness, accountability, and user awareness will be pivotal in harnessing the potential of GANs while minimizing their negative societal impacts. By addressing these ethical dimensions, we can harness the creative potential of GANs to enrich art, innovation, and human-machine collaboration while upholding ethical standards and values.

# CHAPTER 3
# VARIATIONAL AUTOENCODERS (VAES)

In the realm of generative artificial intelligence, Variational Autoencoders (VAEs) stand as a remarkable innovation that bridges the gap between generative models and probabilistic inference. These elegant constructs have revolutionized how machines perceive and generate data, offering a powerful framework for capturing the latent structures and complex patterns within it. Variational Autoencoders, often abbreviated as VAEs, have rapidly gained prominence in fields ranging from computer vision to natural language processing, making them a cornerstone in the ever-expanding toolkit of machine learning practitioners.

At their core, VAEs are a type of generative model that excel at encoding and decoding data. They are fundamentally different from traditional autoencoders, which are primarily used for dimensionality reduction and feature learning. VAEs, on the other hand, introduce a probabilistic twist to the autoencoder architecture, making them not only proficient at compressing data into a lower-dimensional representation but also skilled at generating new data samples that adhere to the underlying statistical patterns of the input data.

This intriguing duality of VAEs—acting as both data encoders and generators—rests on the concept of a latent space, a mathematical construct that represents the essence of the data. VAEs use this latent space to capture the essence of variability within the data, providing a structured and continuous representation of the underlying information. In essence, they distill the essence of data into a compact and meaningful form, making them invaluable for tasks like data compression, denoising, and even creative content generation.

The power of Variational Autoencoders lies not only in their practical applications but also in their theoretical underpinnings. They bring probabilistic modeling into the world of deep learning, allowing for uncertainty estimation and probability distributions over the latent space. This property opens the door to a wide array of applications beyond simple data generation, including anomaly detection, data imputation, and even probabilistic reasoning.

As we embark on a journey to delve deeper into Variational Autoencoders, this exploration will uncover the architecture, training mechanisms, and diverse applications that make VAEs a compelling addition to the toolkit of generative AI. From generating realistic images and text to aiding scientific discovery and medical diagnosis, the versatility of VAEs demonstrates their potential to transform the way we perceive and interact with data in our increasingly data-centric world.

## Comprehensive overview of variational autoencoders

Variational Autoencoders, commonly known as VAEs, are a class of generative models that have gained significant traction in the field of machine learning and artificial intelligence. They combine elements of both probabilistic modeling and neural networks to provide a versatile framework for tasks such as data generation, denoising, and representation learning. In this comprehensive overview, we will explore the architecture, training process, and key concepts behind VAEs.

## Autoencoders:

To understand VAEs, it's essential to grasp the basics of autoencoders. Autoencoders are neural networks designed for dimensionality reduction and feature learning. They consist of two main components: an encoder and a decoder. The encoder maps input data into a lower-dimensional latent space representation, while the decoder attempts to reconstruct the input data from this representation. Autoencoders aim to minimize the reconstruction error, effectively learning a compressed representation of the input data.

## Probabilistic Interpretation:

What sets VAEs apart from traditional autoencoders is their probabilistic interpretation. VAEs model the latent space as a probability distribution, typically assuming it follows a multivariate Gaussian distribution. This probabilistic approach allows VAEs to capture uncertainty and generate data points that are not merely deterministic reconstructions but probabilistic samples from the learned distribution.

**Encoder:**

The encoder network in a VAE takes the input data and maps it to the parameters of the latent space distribution. It consists of several layers of neural networks, often referred to as the recognition network. The encoder network learns to produce two sets of parameters: the mean ($\mu$) and the standard deviation ($\sigma$) of the Gaussian distribution representing the latent space.

**Sampling from Latent Space:**

The crucial step in VAEs is the reparameterization trick. To sample from the latent space distribution efficiently, VAEs use the mean ($\mu$) and standard deviation ($\sigma$) produced by the encoder. Rather than directly sampling from these parameters, which would make backpropagation difficult, VAEs sample from a standard Gaussian distribution (usually $N(0,1)$) and then transform this sample using $\mu$ and $\sigma$ to obtain a sample from the latent space.

**Decoder:**

The decoder network takes samples from the latent space and maps them back to the data space. Like the encoder, it consists of several layers of neural networks. The decoder aims to generate data points that resemble the input data, given the sampled latent space variables.

**Loss Function:**

VAEs are trained using a loss function that consists of two terms: a reconstruction loss and a regularization term. The reconstruction loss measures how well the decoder can reconstruct the input data from the latent space, and it is typically based on a probabilistic measure like the negative log-likelihood. The regularization term, often known as the Kullback-Leibler (KL) divergence, encourages the latent space distribution to be close to a standard Gaussian distribution, effectively regularizing the model.

## Applications:

VAEs find applications in a wide range of domains. They are commonly used for generating realistic images, generating text, and denoising data. Additionally, they are used in anomaly detection, where deviations from the learned latent space distribution indicate anomalies. VAEs have also made significant contributions to the field of reinforcement learning.

## Challenges and Variations:

While VAEs are a powerful tool, they are not without challenges. One common issue is generating data samples that are sometimes less sharp or realistic compared to other generative models like Generative Adversarial Networks (GANs). Researchers have proposed variations of VAEs, such as conditional VAEs and $\beta$-VAEs, to address some of these limitations and introduce additional control over the generated data.

In conclusion, Variational Autoencoders represent a sophisticated approach to generative modeling and probabilistic inference. Their ability to model data as probabilistic distributions in a latent space opens the door to various applications and makes them a valuable addition to the toolbox of machine learning practitioners. Understanding

VAEs is essential for anyone interested in harnessing the creative and data-driven potential of generative AI.

## Encoder and decoder architecture in VAEs

Variational Autoencoders (VAEs) are a class of generative models that employ neural networks for encoding and decoding data. The encoder and decoder are two crucial components that define the architecture of VAEs, enabling them to capture complex data distributions and generate new samples from them. In this detailed explanation, we will explore the intricacies of the encoder and decoder in VAEs.

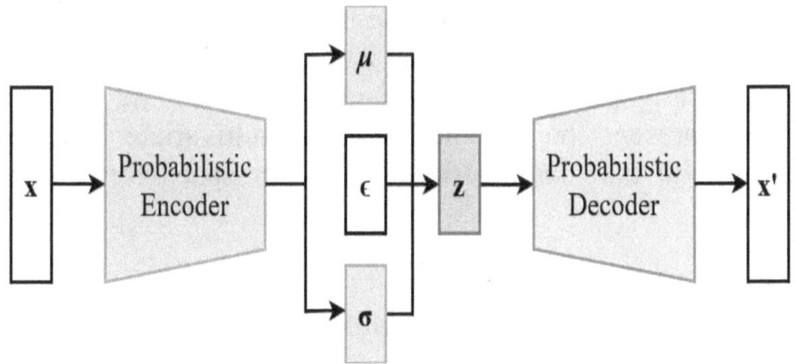


***Pic Credit: Wikipedia***

## Encoder Architecture:

The encoder in a Variational Autoencoder is responsible for mapping input data, often referred to as x, into the latent space representation, which is represented as z. The latent space is where the VAE captures essential features and variability of the data. Here's a breakdown of the components and architecture of the encoder:

**Input Layer:** The encoder starts with an input layer that receives the raw data, which can be images, text, or any other type of data.

**Hidden Layers:** Following the input layer, there are one or more hidden layers consisting of neurons (or nodes) that perform various transformations on the input data. These layers extract hierarchical features from the data.

**Mean ($\mu$) and Standard Deviation ($\sigma$) Layers:** The crucial aspect of the encoder in VAEs is the generation of two sets of parameters for each data point in the latent space: the mean ($\mu$) and the standard deviation ($\sigma$). These parameters are typically produced by separate layers in the encoder. They represent the parameters of a multivariate Gaussian distribution that characterizes the latent space for a given input.

**Sampling Layer:** To sample from the Gaussian distribution defined by $\mu$ and $\sigma$ efficiently, VAEs employ the reparameterization trick. A separate layer in the encoder generates a random sample $\varepsilon$ from a standard Gaussian distribution (usually $N(0,1)$), and this sample is then combined with $\mu$ and $\sigma$ to produce a sample z in the latent space. This step allows for backpropagation during training.

**Decoder Architecture:**

The decoder in a VAE takes the sampled latent space representation z and attempts to generate data that resembles the original input data x. It is responsible for producing data samples, which can be images, text, or other types of data.

Here's a breakdown of the components and architecture of the decoder:

**Input Layer:** The decoder starts with an input layer that takes the sampled latent space representation z.

**Hidden Layers:** Similar to the encoder, the decoder comprises one or more hidden layers that process the latent space representation and gradually transform it to resemble the original data.

**Output Layer:** The final layer of the decoder produces the output data, which aims to resemble the input data x as closely as possible. The architecture of this layer depends on the type of data being generated. For example, in image generation tasks, this layer might consist of multiple neurons, each contributing to a pixel in the generated image.

**Training Process:**

The training of a VAE involves optimizing the model's parameters, including those in the encoder and decoder, to minimize a specific loss function. This loss function typically consists of two terms: a reconstruction loss and a regularization term (Kullback-Leibler divergence). The reconstruction loss measures how well the decoder can reconstruct the input data, while the regularization term encourages the latent space distribution to be close to a standard Gaussian distribution.

By iteratively adjusting the encoder and decoder parameters during training, the VAE learns to capture the underlying data distribution in the latent space, enabling it to generate new data samples that resemble the training data.

In conclusion, the encoder and decoder architectures in Variational Autoencoders are fundamental components that allow these models to capture and generate complex data distributions. The encoder maps input data into a structured latent space, while the decoder generates data samples from this latent space. Together, they enable VAEs to perform tasks such as data generation, denoising, and representation learning, making them a valuable tool in the field of generative artificial intelligence.

**Latent space and its role in generating new data**

The concept of the latent space is at the heart of many generative models, including Variational Autoencoders (VAEs) and Generative Adversarial Networks (GANs). The latent space is a crucial component that plays a central role in capturing data representations and generating new, meaningful data. In this detailed explanation, we will delve into what the latent space is and how it facilitates the generation of new data.

**What is the Latent Space?**

The latent space is a mathematical construct within a generative model that represents a lower-dimensional space where data is encoded in a structured and meaningful way. It is an abstract space where each point corresponds to a different data representation. In simpler terms, it's a space where data can be represented in a more compact form while retaining the essential information needed to recreate the original data.

**Role of the Latent Space:**

Dimensionality Reduction: One of the primary roles of the latent space is dimensionality reduction. In many real-world datasets, especially in fields like computer vision and natural language processing, data can be incredibly high-dimensional. The latent space provides a lower-dimensional representation that captures the most important features and patterns within the data. This dimensionality reduction not only saves computational resources but also aids in data compression and storage.

**Capturing Variability:** The latent space serves as a repository for capturing the inherent variability present in the data. Each point in the latent space represents a different configuration or variation of the data. For instance, in image data, the latent space can capture variations in style, color, and content. This enables the generative model to produce diverse and realistic data samples by sampling different points in the latent space.

**Interpolation:** Because the latent space is continuous and structured, it allows for meaningful interpolation between data points. By smoothly transitioning between two points in the latent space, the generative model can generate data that gradually change from one data instance to another. This is often used for tasks like image morphing or generating sequences of data with smooth transitions.

**Data Generation:** The latent space is the foundation for generating new data samples. In generative models like VAEs and GANs, the decoder (or generator) network takes points from the latent space and transforms them into data samples. By providing different points from the latent space as input to the decoder, you can generate diverse data samples that follow the same patterns and distributions as the training data.

**Representation Learning:** The latent space also facilitates representation learning. The encoder network in VAEs learns to map input data to the latent space. This means that data is transformed into a structured and meaningful representation within the latent space. These representations can be useful for downstream tasks such as classification, clustering, or anomaly detection.

In summary, the latent space is a critical concept in generative models, enabling them to capture and manipulate data representations effectively. It serves as a compact, structured, and interpretable space where data can be transformed and generated. The latent space's role in dimensionality reduction, capturing variability, interpolation, data generation, and representation learning makes it a foundational component in the field of generative artificial intelligence.

**Use cases: image generation, anomaly detection, molecular design**

Variational Autoencoders (VAEs) have demonstrated their versatility across a wide range of applications, thanks to their ability to learn meaningful representations of data in a probabilistic manner. In this detailed explanation, we will explore three diverse use cases where VAEs have made significant contributions: image generation, anomaly detection, and molecular design.

## 1. Image Generation:

VAEs have proven to be powerful tools for generating realistic and diverse images. This use case has found applications in various domains, including art, entertainment, and computer vision. Here's how VAEs excel in image generation:

**Artistic Creations:** VAEs can learn the underlying patterns and structures in a dataset of images, allowing them to generate entirely new and creative artwork. Artists and designers have used VAEs to generate unique visuals, often blending different styles, themes, or content to produce original pieces of art.

**Data Augmentation:** In machine learning, having a large and diverse dataset is crucial for training robust models. VAEs can be employed to augment existing datasets by generating new, synthetic data samples that are similar to the original data. This is particularly useful for tasks like object recognition and classification.

**Style Transfer:** VAEs can learn to separate content and style from images. This separation allows for intriguing applications such as style transfer, where the style of one image can be applied to the content of another, resulting in visually appealing and creative compositions.

## 2. Anomaly Detection:

Anomaly detection is a critical task in various fields, including finance, cybersecurity, and quality control. VAEs can be leveraged to identify unusual or anomalous data points in a dataset:

**Fraud Detection:** In finance, VAEs can learn the normal patterns of financial transactions and detect unusual behavior that may indicate fraud or malicious activity. Anomalies in transaction data, such as unusual spending patterns, can trigger alerts for further investigation.

**Network Security:** VAEs can be applied to network traffic data to detect unusual patterns of communication that may suggest a cyberattack or intrusion. Deviations from typical network behavior can be flagged as potential security threats.

**Manufacturing Quality Control:** In manufacturing, VAEs can be used to monitor the quality of products on assembly lines. Anomalies in product specifications, such as dimensions or surface defects, can be detected in real-time, ensuring product quality.


## 3. Molecular Design:

VAEs have made significant contributions to computational chemistry and drug discovery by aiding in the design of molecules with specific properties:

**De Novo Drug Design:** VAEs can generate molecular structures with desired properties, making them valuable tools in drug discovery. Researchers can input specific molecular properties or targets, and VAEs can produce molecules that match these criteria. This accelerates the process of drug discovery by suggesting potential candidates for further study.

**Materials Science:** VAEs can also be applied in materials science to design new materials with desired properties, such as electrical conductivity, strength, or thermal stability. Researchers can input the properties they need, and VAEs can suggest molecular structures that exhibit these characteristics.

**Quantum Chemistry:** In quantum chemistry, VAEs can assist in exploring the vast chemical space of molecular configurations. They can be used to generate diverse sets of molecular structures for quantum simulations, enabling the study of chemical reactions and properties.

In conclusion, Variational Autoencoders (VAEs) have demonstrated their versatility in a wide array of applications, including image generation, anomaly detection, and molecular design. Their ability to learn probabilistic representations of data, capture complex patterns, and generate new, meaningful data points has made them indispensable tools in fields ranging from art and cybersecurity to pharmaceutical research and materials science. VAEs continue to push the boundaries of what is possible in generative modeling and data analysis.

# CHAPTER 4
# TEXT GENERATION AND NATURAL LANGUAGE PROCESSING

In the realm of Generative AI, the power to generate human-like text is a testament to the ingenuity of technology. Chapter 3 delves into the intricate world of Text Generation and Natural Language Processing (NLP), where machines grasp the subtleties of language, harnessing words to create narratives, dialogues, and prose. As we step into this chapter, we embark on a journey through the algorithms, models, and techniques that enable machines to not only comprehend human language but also craft coherent, contextually relevant text. From automatic summarization to dialogue generation, from language translation to creative writing, we explore the myriad ways in which Text Generation and NLP are revolutionizing communication, enabling cross-cultural understanding, and even blurring the lines between human and machine-generated prose. As we delve into the heart of this chapter, we uncover the symbiotic relationship between linguistics, technology, and imagination, unraveling the intricate mechanisms that transform mere words into vehicles of thought, connection, and expression.

## Language models and their role in text generation

In the landscape of Text Generation and Natural Language Processing (NLP), language models stand as the cornerstone of machines' ability to understand, process, and generate human-like text. These models represent the culmination of decades of research, leveraging vast amounts of textual data to learn the intricate patterns and structures that characterize human language. Their role is pivotal in transforming AI from a mere rule-based responder to a sophisticated communicator that can generate contextually relevant, coherent, and often creative text.

## Understanding Language Models:

Language models are algorithms that learn the statistical properties of language from extensive text corpora. They learn to predict the likelihood of a sequence of words occurring based on the patterns they've observed in the training data. This ability to predict the next word in a sequence allows language models to grasp grammar, syntax, and semantics, enabling them to generate text that mirrors the linguistic structures found in human communication.

## Types of Language Models:

Language models come in various flavors, with two primary categories being n-gram models and neural language models. N-gram models analyze sequences of n consecutive words, while neural language models employ deep learning techniques, often in the form of recurrent neural networks (RNNs) or transformer-based architectures.

## Role in Text Generation:

Language models serve as the creative engines of text generation. Given a prompt or a starting sentence, these models generate subsequent text by predicting the most probable next word based on the context provided. The generated text flows naturally, adhering to the linguistic rules and patterns they've internalized during training.

## Challenges in Text Generation:

While language models have made remarkable strides in text generation, they also face challenges. They can sometimes produce text that's grammatically correct but lacks coherence or context. Ensuring that the generated text remains coherent, contextually relevant, and free from biases or harmful content is an ongoing endeavor in the field.

## Advancements and Applications:

Recent advancements in language models, particularly with the introduction of transformer architectures like BERT, GPT, and their variants, have revolutionized text generation. These models have found applications in machine translation, summarization, question-answering, chatbots, and even creative writing. They've bridged the gap between human and machine communication, enabling AI to participate in conversations, assist in content creation, and enhance information retrieval.

**Ethical Considerations:**

The power of language models also raises ethical concerns, particularly in generating fake news, harmful content, or biased language. Ensuring that language models are trained on diverse and representative data and implementing mechanisms to prevent misuse is essential in responsible AI deployment.

In the realm of Text Generation and NLP, language models are the linchpin that enables machines to traverse the intricate nuances of human communication. Their role as linguistic scholars and creative storytellers illuminates the potential of AI to become a co-author in the narrative of human expression.

## Recurrent Neural Networks (RNNs) and Long Short-Term Memory (LSTM) networks.

In the realm of Natural Language Processing (NLP) and sequential data analysis, Recurrent Neural Networks (RNNs) and their advanced variant, Long Short-Term Memory (LSTM) networks, stand as transformative architectures that enable machines to grasp the contextual dynamics of sequences. These networks are designed to process sequences of data, making them indispensable for tasks like text generation, language translation, sentiment analysis, and more.

## Recurrent Neural Networks (RNNs): Modeling Sequential Dependencies

At the heart of RNNs lies the notion of recurrence—a network architecture that feeds the output of a previous step back as input to the current step. This cyclic nature allows

RNNs to capture sequential dependencies, enabling them to understand the context and relationships between different elements in a sequence. However, standard RNNs suffer from vanishing and exploding gradient problems, which hinder their capacity to capture long-range dependencies.

## Long Short-Term Memory (LSTM) Networks: Preserving Context and Memory

LSTM networks are an evolution of RNNs that tackle the limitations of vanishing gradients and address the challenge of learning long-term dependencies. LSTMs introduce specialized memory cells and gating mechanisms that allow them to selectively store, update, and forget information. These components include the input gate (which determines what information to store), the forget gate (which decides what information to discard), and the output gate (which controls the information passed to the next step). This dynamic memory allocation and gating mechanism enable LSTMs to retain context over long sequences, making them particularly adept at capturing intricate linguistic patterns in language data.

## Applications in NLP:

RNNs and LSTMs have found a myriad of applications in NLP. They excel in tasks like sentiment analysis, where the sentiment of a text is determined based on the order of words. They are employed in language modeling, where they predict the next word in a sequence given the preceding words. Additionally, they play a crucial role in machine translation, where they align and translate words between different languages while maintaining context.

**Challenges and Advancements:**

Despite their capabilities, RNNs and LSTMs face challenges in processing extremely long sequences and capturing complex dependencies. The introduction of attention mechanisms and transformer architectures has pushed the boundaries of sequence modeling further, allowing for parallel processing and capturing global context more effectively.

**In Summation:**

RNNs and LSTMs are foundational architectures in NLP that enable machines to navigate the intricacies of sequential data. They form the bedrock of various NLP tasks, empowering AI systems to generate coherent text, understand context, and make sense of the nuanced relationships embedded within language. While they've paved the way for significant advancements, they're also a testament to the ever-evolving nature of AI, as newer architectures like transformers continue to reshape the landscape of sequence modeling.

**Transformers Architecture: Understanding Attention Mechanisms**

The Transformers architecture stands as a revolutionary milestone in Natural Language Processing (NLP), redefining how machines comprehend and generate sequential data like text. At the core of this architecture lies a powerful concept known as attention mechanisms—a mechanism inspired by human cognitive processes. Transformers have revolutionized tasks like machine translation, text generation, and sentiment analysis, elevating the capabilities of AI systems to understand and generate language with unprecedented accuracy and fluency.

## Attention Mechanism: Emulating Human Focus

The attention mechanism in Transformers is inspired by how humans focus on specific parts of a text or context while understanding or generating language. Just as we give varying levels of importance to different words when comprehending a sentence, attention mechanisms allow the model to assign varying degrees of relevance to different parts of the input text when generating an output word.

## Self-Attention: Weighing Words in Context

In Transformers, self-attention enables the model to weigh the importance of each word in the input sequence with respect to every other word. This process generates attention scores that reflect the significance of each word in relation to the context. These attention scores are then used to compute a weighted sum of the input sequence, which encapsulates the context that a specific word should consider.

## Multi-Head Attention: Capturing Different Aspects

Transformers extend self-attention to multi-head attention, allowing the model to capture different aspects of context. Multiple attention mechanisms operate in parallel, each focusing on different relationships within the input sequence. This parallelism enables the model to capture various types of dependencies and nuances present in the text.

## Positional Encodings: Encoding Sequence Information

Since the attention mechanism doesn't inherently consider the order of words, positional encodings are added to the input embeddings. These encodings provide the model with information about the position of each word in the sequence. By combining the embeddings and positional encodings, the model can capture both the content and the sequence information, enabling it to understand context-rich relationships.

## Advantages of Transformers:

Transformers have several advantages over traditional sequence models like Recurrent Neural Networks (RNNs) and Long Short-Term Memory (LSTM) networks. They can process sequences in parallel, making them highly efficient. They can also capture long-range dependencies effectively, thanks to self-attention's global context understanding. This makes them particularly adept at handling tasks that involve understanding and generating language with complex contextual dependencies.

## Applications and Impact:

Transformers have significantly impacted NLP. Models like BERT, GPT, and their variants have achieved state-of-the-art results in various tasks, from language translation to question-answering. They've paved the way for zero-shot learning, where models can perform tasks they haven't been explicitly trained on. This demonstrates the remarkable ability of attention-based Transformers to generalize and understand the nuances of language.

## Applications of AI-generated text: content creation, dialogue systems, and language translation

The advancements in Natural Language Processing (NLP) and Generative AI have unlocked a world of possibilities for AI-generated text across various domains. From generating captivating stories to facilitating conversations and breaking language barriers, AI-generated text has permeated industries, transforming the way we communicate, create, and connect.

## Content Creation: Unlocking Creativity and Efficiency

AI-generated text has reshaped the landscape of content creation. Automated writing tools powered by language models have been employed to produce articles, blogs, marketing copy, and product descriptions. They assist writers by suggesting relevant content, optimizing language, and even generating entire paragraphs. These tools streamline the content creation process, freeing up human writers to focus on higher-level creative tasks.

## Dialogue Systems: Conversing with Machines

Dialogue systems, often referred to as chatbots or virtual assistants, have become integral to customer service and user interaction. AI-generated text empowers these systems to engage in natural-sounding conversations, answering queries, providing information, and even assisting with tasks. Through a blend of predefined responses and real-time generation, dialogue systems enable seamless human-machine interactions in customer support, healthcare, education, and more.

## Language Translation: Bridging Global Communication

AI-generated text has transformed language translation, making cross-cultural communication more accessible. Neural machine translation models, often based on transformer architectures, can translate text between languages with remarkable fluency and accuracy. They've enabled real-time translation in applications like travel, international business, and online content consumption. AI-powered translation tools empower individuals and businesses to transcend linguistic boundaries.

## Content Summarization: Distilling Information

AI-generated text excels in content summarization, distilling lengthy documents into concise, coherent summaries. These summaries provide readers with the essence of the content, making it easier to comprehend and extract key information. Applications range from summarizing news articles for quick updates to condensing lengthy research papers for efficient information consumption.

## Text Generation for Creativity: Art and Music

AI-generated text isn't confined to utilitarian applications it's also a tool for artistic expression. Language models have been used to generate poetry, stories, and even scripts for plays. Beyond written text, AI has delved into music composition, creating melodies, harmonies, and lyrics that evoke emotions and resonate with listeners. This fusion of technology and creativity redefines the boundaries of human-machine collaboration.

## Ethical Considerations:

While AI-generated text offers a plethora of benefits, it also raises ethical considerations. The potential for misinformation, copyright infringement, and the amplification of biases present in training data are challenges that need to be addressed to ensure responsible and ethical use of AI-generated text.

## The Future Landscape:

As AI-generated text becomes more integrated into our lives, it will continue to transform industries, enhance communication, and reshape creative processes. With ongoing research and development, AI-generated text has the potential to further refine its capabilities, understanding nuances, context, and human intent, ultimately leading to more natural and empathetic interactions between humans and machines.

# CHAPTER 5
# IMAGE AND ART GENERATION

In the digital age, the marriage of technology and artistic expression has birthed a captivating realm known as the Image and Art Generation. This innovative field harnesses the computational prowess of artificial intelligence to breathe life into pixels, producing visuals that blur the boundaries between human creativity and machine ingenuity. From paintings that evoke emotions to landscapes that transport us to uncharted realms, Image and Art Generation showcases the transformative potential of algorithms in shaping the visual arts.

**Exploring the Canvas of Possibilities:**

In this chapter, we delve into the enchanting world where code and pixels converge to create visual narratives that resonate with audiences across the globe. From mastering the techniques of classical art to pioneering groundbreaking styles that challenge convention, AI's foray into image and art generation expands the horizons of what is achievable through creative collaboration between humans and machines. As we navigate the intricate brushwork of neural networks, we unravel how these algorithms decipher the essence of visual aesthetics, empowering technology to become a canvas for human expression and imagination.

## Generating art with neural style transfer

Neural Style Transfer (NST) is a remarkable technique that marries the world of artificial intelligence and artistic expression, allowing for the creation of captivating artworks that blend the content of one image with the stylistic features of another. This fusion of content and style has given rise to a fascinating method of generating unique and aesthetically pleasing artworks that cater to the preferences of both human creators and machine algorithms.

## Understanding the Process:

At its core, neural style transfer involves two key components: the content image and the style image. The content image is the base on which the artwork is built, providing the underlying subject and structure. The style image, on the other hand, contributes the visual aesthetic and artistic flair that define the final output. The goal is to transform the content image in a way that preserves its underlying subject while imbuing it with the stylistic characteristics of the chosen style image.

## The Role of Neural Networks:

Neural networks play a pivotal role in NST, particularly convolutional neural networks (CNNs). CNNs excel at capturing the intricate features and patterns present in images, making them well-suited for analyzing both content and style. The content image is fed through the network to extract its high-level features, while the style image similarly undergoes analysis to capture its artistic characteristics. By manipulating the content image based on the features extracted from the style image, the algorithm reconstructs an image that seamlessly merges both content and style.

## Loss Functions and Optimization:

The magic of neural style transfer lies in the formulation of loss functions. Multiple loss functions are used to quantify how well the generated image preserves content and mimics style. These loss functions include content loss, which measures the difference between the features of the generated image and the content image, and style loss, which captures the difference in the statistical properties of the generated and style images. An optimization process then iteratively adjusts the generated image to minimize these loss functions, refining its content and style representation.

## Applications and Creative Exploration:

Neural style transfer transcends mere algorithms; it empowers artists, creators, and enthusiasts to explore new horizons of visual expression. By experimenting with different content and style images, one can generate a diverse range of artworks—transforming photographs into paintings inspired by famous artists, merging the aesthetics of different eras, and even crafting novel visual experiences that challenge conventions.


## The Intersection of Art and Technology:

Neural style transfer exemplifies the harmonious intersection of art and technology. It not only showcases the computational prowess of neural networks but also encapsulates the essence of artistic interpretation. This technique allows artists and enthusiasts to reimagine traditional styles, fuse different visual languages, and sculpt images that resonate with emotion and innovation. Neural style transfer epitomizes the potential of AI as a creative collaborator, redefining the canvas of artistic creation.


## Creating realistic images using GANs

Generative Adversarial Networks (GANs) have revolutionized the field of image generation, enabling the creation of highly realistic and visually captivating images. GANs are a class of neural networks that consist of two main components: a generator and a discriminator. The interplay between these components leads to the generation of images that are often indistinguishable from real photographs. This advancement in AI-generated images has found applications in various industries, including art, entertainment, design, and even scientific research.


## Generator-Discriminator Dance:

The generator network in a GAN is responsible for creating images. It starts with random noise and progressively transforms it into images by learning from a dataset of real images during the training process. The discriminator network, on the other hand, acts as a detective, differentiating between real images and those generated by the generator. The training process involves a back-and-forth exchange: the generator strives to create images that deceive the discriminator, while the discriminator refines its ability to distinguish between real and generated images. Over time, this adversarial dynamic leads to the generation of increasingly realistic images.

## Loss Functions and Training:

The training process of GANs involves optimizing loss functions for both the generator and the discriminator. The generator aims to minimize a loss function that penalizes it for producing images that the discriminator can easily identify as fake. Conversely, the discriminator aims to minimize a loss function that quantifies its ability to differentiate between real and fake images. This tug-of-war between the generator and the discriminator fosters a convergence point where the generator creates images that closely mimic the distribution of real images.

## Applications in Realism:

The ability of GANs to create realistic images has opened the doors to numerous applications. In the world of art, GANs have been employed to create digital paintings, sculptures, and even entire virtual worlds. In design and architecture, GANs can generate photorealistic building facades and interior designs, aiding architects in visualization. The entertainment industry has also embraced GAN-generated characters, environments, and visual effects, enhancing cinematic experiences. Moreover, GANs have been utilized in scientific research to generate realistic images for data augmentation, aiding the training of machine learning models.

## The Art of Blurring Reality:

Creating realistic images using GANs represents a captivating fusion of artistic creativity and computational prowess. These AI-generated images blur the line between human creation and machine innovation, showcasing the potential of GANs to reshape visual aesthetics across industries and redefine our perception of realism in the digital realm.

## Case studies: DALL-E and the fusion of text and images

DALL-E, a groundbreaking creation of the Generative Adversarial Network (GAN) era, has emerged as a transformative example of how AI can seamlessly blend the realms of text and images, pushing the boundaries of creativity and imagination to unprecedented heights. Developed by OpenAI, DALL-E showcases the remarkable potential of GANs to synthesize images based on textual prompts, thereby bridging the gap between linguistic expression and visual representation.

## Understanding DALL-E's Innovation:

DALL-E's innovation lies in its ability to generate images from textual descriptions. Users provide prompts in the form of sentences describing what they envision, and DALL-E translates these descriptions into stunning, original images that align with the given prompts. This remarkable fusion of text and image generation not only showcases AI's ability to understand context and semantics but also reveals its capacity to conjure visuals that align with human-inspired concepts.

## The Technical Marvel:

DALL-E's architecture is a variant of the GAN framework, with a generator network that transforms textual embeddings into images and a discriminator network that evaluates the realism of the generated images. The generator is trained to produce images that not only match the textual descriptions but also exhibit high visual fidelity. This process involves iterative optimization, where the generator refines its output in response to feedback from the discriminator, resulting in images that progressively become more coherent, creative, and aligned with the prompts.

## Creative Potential and Applications:

DALL-E's creative potential is virtually limitless. It can generate images based on textual prompts ranging from concrete descriptions to abstract concepts. The generated images span a wide spectrum, from familiar objects and animals to surreal and imaginative scenes. This versatility has sparked interest across multiple domains, including art, design, advertising, and storytelling. DALL-E has been used to create visually stunning book covers, illustrate fantastical creatures, and even visualize abstract philosophical concepts.

## Challenges and Ethical Considerations:

DALL-E's capabilities also raise ethical considerations, particularly in terms of its potential to produce content that is biased, inappropriate, or misaligned with societal norms. Ensuring that AI-generated content adheres to ethical standards and guidelines is a critical concern when deploying DALL-E and similar technologies.

## Impact on Human Creativity:

DALL-E showcases the symbiotic relationship between AI and human creativity. It doesn't replace human artists or creators but serves as a collaborator, generating ideas and visuals that can spark new artistic directions. Artists can use DALL-E as a source of inspiration, building upon the generated content to create unique pieces that blend human ingenuity with machine-generated suggestions.

## Conclusion: Redefining Creative Collaboration:

DALL-E's fusion of text and image generation stands as a testament to the harmonious collaboration between language and visuals, human and machine. This case study illuminates AI's potential not only to replicate patterns but also to synthesize novel concepts and push the envelope of human creativity. As DALL-E continues to evolve, it highlights the transformative role AI can play in enhancing artistic expression, communication, and the dynamic interaction between words and images.

## Copyright and ownership issues in AI-generated art

The emergence of AI-generated art has given rise to a complex and evolving landscape of copyright and ownership issues. As machines contribute to the creative process, questions arise regarding who holds the rights to AI-generated artworks, how copyright law applies to them, and what ethical considerations must be taken into account. This intersection of technology and art has prompted legal and ethical discussions that shape the future of creative expression.

## Originality and Authorship:

Copyright law typically grants protection to original works created by human authors. However, the concept of "authorship" becomes convoluted in the realm of AI-generated art. While the AI system executes the creative process, it's often a result of human programming, training data, and algorithms. Determining whether an AI system can be considered an "author" under copyright law challenges traditional notions of creativity and ownership.

## AI as a Tool vs. Creator:

One viewpoint posits that AI should be treated as a tool or toolset used by human creators, similar to brushes and canvases. In this context, the human programmer or artist who designs, trains, and guides the AI system may hold the copyright to the generated artwork. However, this approach overlooks the fact that AI systems can produce novel and unexpected outcomes that diverge from human intent.

## Lack of Human Creative Input:

Some AI-generated artworks are produced without explicit human creative input. In these cases, where an AI system independently generates artworks without human intervention, determining authorship becomes even more complex. Should these works be considered in the public domain, or should a new legal framework be established to accommodate these scenarios?

## Licensing and Usage Rights:

In cases where copyright is attributed to human creators, licensing and usage rights need to be carefully considered. Artists might choose to license AI-generated works for specific uses or limit their distribution. However, the lack of traditional human artistic intent can complicate the determination of appropriate licensing terms and usage restrictions.

## Ethical Concerns:

Beyond legal considerations, ethical questions arise. How do we ensure AI-generated artworks are free from bias and harmful content? How do we address issues of cultural appropriation or misrepresentation that AI systems might perpetuate? Ethical frameworks that govern AI art creation and usage need to be developed in tandem with legal norms.

## Future Frameworks:

Addressing copyright and ownership issues in AI-generated art requires collaborative efforts among legal experts, artists, ethicists, and AI developers. Some propose creating new legal designations for AI-generated content, such as "co-creators" that acknowledge both human and machine contributions. International discussions are crucial to formulating frameworks that align copyright law with the evolving nature of creative collaboration.

## Balancing Innovation and Protection:

The evolving landscape of copyright and ownership in AI-generated art highlights the delicate balance between fostering innovation and protecting the rights of creators. As AI-generated art continues to shape artistic expression, collaborative models that respect the contributions of both humans and machines will be instrumental in ensuring a harmonious and equitable future for art and technology.

# CHAPTER 6
# MUSIC AND AUDIO COMPOSITION

In the symphony of technological progress, the realms of Music and Audio Composition have experienced a transformative crescendo, marked by the integration of artificial intelligence and artistic ingenuity. This chapter invites us to explore the harmonious fusion of technology and musical creativity, as algorithms join composers and musicians in crafting melodies, harmonies, and rhythms that evoke emotions and transcend traditional boundaries.

From generating innovative compositions to enhancing audio production, AI has become a dynamic collaborator, expanding the horizons of musical creation and auditory experiences. As we delve into the world of Music and Audio Composition, we embark on a melodic journey that resonates with the chords of innovation, highlighting the extraordinary potential of AI to amplify human expression and reimagine the language of sound.

## AI-generated music: from classical to contemporary genres

The fusion of artificial intelligence and music composition has ushered in a new era of creativity, enabling machines to compose melodies, harmonies, and rhythms that span the spectrum of musical genres, from classical to contemporary. AI-generated music stands at the crossroads of innovation and tradition, reshaping the landscape of music production, exploration, and appreciation.

## Understanding the Process:

AI-generated music involves the application of machine learning techniques to analyze existing musical compositions and then create new pieces that reflect similar styles, structures, and characteristics. This process often entails training AI models on extensive datasets of musical scores, exposing them to the complexities of musical patterns, scales, chords, and progressions. The trained models then use this knowledge to generate original compositions, drawing inspiration from the vast repertoire of human-created music.

## Classical Reflections:

In the realm of classical music, AI-generated compositions pay homage to the great composers of the past while introducing innovative twists. AI can produce compositions in the style of renowned composers like Mozart, Beethoven, or Bach, capturing the nuances that define their musical signatures. These compositions evoke a sense of nostalgia while presenting a modern interpretation of classical motifs.

**Contemporary Creativity:**

AI's creative prowess extends beyond classical genres, embracing contemporary styles like pop, jazz, electronic, and even experimental genres. AI models can craft catchy melodies and intricate chord progressions characteristic of pop music. They can produce the improvisational riffs and syncopations of jazz. In the realm of electronic music, AI-generated tracks push sonic boundaries with unconventional rhythms and textures. The adaptability of AI allows it to explore and reinvent the ever-evolving landscape of modern music.

**Collaborative Potential:**

AI-generated music isn't replacing human composers; rather, it serves as a collaborator that sparks inspiration and assists in the creative process. Musicians can use AI-generated compositions as a foundation, building upon them to add their personal touch, instrumental arrangements, and emotional nuances. This collaborative model between humans and machines redefines artistic authorship and the boundaries of creative partnership.

**Challenges and Opportunities:**

While AI-generated music opens doors to innovation, it also presents challenges. Ensuring that the music maintains originality, evokes emotion, and avoids repetitive patterns is a constant endeavor. Moreover, AI-generated music often lacks the intentionality and emotional depth that human composers infuse into their works. Balancing the technical aspects of AI with the artistic essence of music remains a dynamic pursuit.

## The Ongoing Symphony:

AI-generated music exemplifies the dynamic interplay between technology and artistic expression. It offers a canvas for composers, producers, and musicians to explore new horizons and experiment with creative boundaries. As AI continues to refine its understanding of musical intricacies and nuances, it augments the global repertoire of compositions, adding harmonies that speak to both the nostalgia of tradition and the innovation of the future.

## Recurrent neural networks for music composition

Recurrent Neural Networks (RNNs) have emerged as a powerful tool in the realm of music composition, enabling the creation of melodies, harmonies, and rhythms that capture the essence of different musical genres and styles. RNNs excel at processing sequential data, making them well-suited for tasks that involve the temporal and structural intricacies of music. This technology has redefined how composers and musicians approach the creative process, offering new ways to explore and generate musical pieces.

## Modeling Sequential Patterns:

At the core of RNNs lies the ability to capture sequential patterns in data. In the context of music, these patterns encompass the succession of notes, chords, and rhythms that define a musical piece. RNNs process each input (note or chord) in the sequence while maintaining a hidden state that encodes the context of previously encountered inputs. This sequential modeling allows RNNs to generate coherent and melodically satisfying compositions.

**Long Short-Term Memory (LSTM) Networks:**

LSTM networks are a variant of RNNs that excel at capturing long-range dependencies in sequential data. This is crucial in music composition, where melodies and harmonies often span across multiple measures. LSTMs introduce memory cells and gating mechanisms that enable them to selectively store, update, and forget information. These components preserve context over longer sequences, making them particularly adept at generating music with nuanced and intricate patterns.

**Training and Creativity:**

Training an RNN for music composition involves exposing the model to a dataset of existing musical compositions. The model learns the patterns, chord progressions, and stylistic elements present in the data. Once trained, the RNN can generate new music by sampling from the learned distributions of notes and chords. This creative aspect of RNNs allows composers and musicians to explore novel melodies and harmonies, experimenting with variations and stylistic interpretations.

**Incorporating Musical Theory:**

RNNs can be enhanced by incorporating musical theory into the training process. For example, composers can guide the model by specifying a key, tempo, or certain melodic motifs. This way, RNNs produce compositions that adhere to specific musical rules while still exhibiting creative twists. The synergy between AI-generated sequences and human-defined constraints fosters a collaborative and adaptive approach to music composition.

**Beyond Imitation:**

RNNs have the ability to imitate existing musical styles, but they can also be trained to generate hybrid compositions that blend elements from multiple genres. This amalgamation of styles adds a layer of uniqueness to AI-generated music, pushing the boundaries of creativity and challenging traditional musical categorizations.

**The Future of Composition:**

Recurrent Neural Networks for music composition mark a confluence of technological innovation and artistic creativity. They augment the creative process by offering inspiration, suggesting new directions, and providing composers with a new toolbox of musical ideas. As AI continues to evolve, RNNs hold the potential to bridge the gap between traditional and contemporary music, fostering collaborations that redefine the landscape of musical expression.

**Generating audio with WaveGAN and NSynth**

WaveGAN and NSynth are two pioneering techniques that harness the power of deep learning to generate audio waveforms, revolutionizing the field of sound synthesis and composition. These methods delve into the intricate realm of audio generation, transforming raw data into rich and expressive auditory experiences that span diverse genres and sonic landscapes.

**WaveGAN: Unveiling the Sonic Spectrum**

WaveGAN, short for "Waveform Generative Adversarial Network," is an innovative approach to audio generation based on the principles of Generative Adversarial Networks (GANs). GANs consist of a generator and a discriminator network that engage in an adversarial training process. In the context of audio, the generator crafts synthetic audio waveforms, while the discriminator assesses the realism of both real and generated audio. This dynamic adversarial dance propels the generator to produce increasingly authentic audio, ultimately resulting in a sound that can mimic the intricacies of human-created compositions.

## NSynth: Synthesizing New Soundscapes

NSynth, an abbreviation for "Neural Synthesizer," extends the boundaries of audio generation by leveraging deep neural networks to create entirely new sounds that transcend the constraints of traditional instruments. NSynth's foundation lies in autoencoders and generative models, which are trained on a vast collection of real-world instrument sounds. This training allows NSynth to interpolate between different sounds, enabling it to produce entirely novel audio textures that blend elements of existing instruments. The result is a sonic palette that offers a novel form of auditory creativity, generating sounds that may be previously unheard in the realm of music.

## Training and Creative Exploration:

Both WaveGAN and NSynth require substantial training on diverse audio datasets. WaveGAN, for instance, involves training on large collections of real-world audio samples to capture the nuances of different musical styles and genres. NSynth, on the other hand, is trained on individual notes from various instruments, enabling it to interpolate between these notes and create new sonic possibilities. Composers, musicians, and sound designers can use these models as a springboard for creative exploration, generating unique audio textures that add depth and innovation to their projects.

## Applications and Impacts:

WaveGAN and NSynth have profound implications across multiple domains. Musicians can use these techniques to create synthetic instrument sounds, enhancing their musical compositions with a customized sonic palette. Sound designers can generate unique sound effects for multimedia productions, from movies to video games. Moreover, these techniques facilitate the exploration of auditory landscapes that push the boundaries of human auditory perception, leading to artistic innovation and new forms of sonic expression.

## Challenges and Future Directions:

While WaveGAN and NSynth offer groundbreaking opportunities, they also face challenges in capturing the full range of complexity present in human-created audio. Balancing realism, coherence, and diversity in generated audio remains an ongoing pursuit. The development of techniques that account for nuances like emotional expression, timbral variations, and dynamic changes within audio will further enrich the capabilities of these models.

## The Sonic Frontier:

WaveGAN and NSynth exemplify the dynamic marriage of technology and artistic expression in the realm of audio generation. They open doors to sonic creativity, reshaping how musicians, composers, and sound enthusiasts approach audio composition and manipulation. As these techniques continue to evolve, they expand the auditory horizons, offering a symphony of possibilities that redefine our understanding of sound and its limitless potential.

## The role of AI in assisting musicians and composers

Artificial Intelligence (AI) has emerged as a transformative force in the realm of music, enhancing the creative process and expanding the horizons of musicians and composers. Rather than replacing human creativity, AI serves as a collaborative partner, offering tools, insights, and inspiration that augment artistic expression and redefine the boundaries of musical composition.

## Musical Composition and Generation:

AI has demonstrated remarkable capabilities in generating musical compositions. By training on vast datasets of existing music, AI models can produce original melodies, harmonies, and rhythms that align with specific genres or styles. Composers can use AI-generated compositions as starting points, experimenting with variations, harmonizations, and instrumentations to craft unique musical pieces that bear their personal touch.

## Creative Inspiration:

AI-generated music serves as a wellspring of inspiration. Musicians can use AI models to explore new chord progressions, melodic motifs, or rhythmic patterns that they might not have considered otherwise. This collaborative brainstorming with AI sparks novel ideas and encourages musicians to venture beyond their comfort zones, enriching their creative output.

## Generating Accompaniments and Arrangements:

AI excels at producing accompanying parts and arrangements that complement a melody or theme. Musicians can input a melody, and AI algorithms can create harmonies, counter-melodies, and accompaniments that harmonically enrich the piece. This capability is particularly valuable for songwriters and composers seeking to flesh out their musical ideas into full arrangements.

## Style Imitation and Fusion:

AI's ability to imitate specific musical styles offers composers the chance to experiment with diverse genres and eras. Composers can create compositions inspired by classical, jazz, pop, or even experimental styles, enabling them to explore new realms of musical expression. AI's capacity to fuse different styles also pushes the boundaries of genre, leading to innovative compositions that blend influences from various musical traditions.

## Instant Feedback and Iteration:

AI provides real-time feedback during the composition process. Musicians can input their musical ideas, and AI models can instantly provide suggestions, identify dissonances, or suggest variations. This iterative feedback loop accelerates the creative process, allowing musicians to refine their compositions with agility and efficiency.

## Customized Soundscapes:

AI's impact extends to sound design and production. Musicians can use AI algorithms to create custom instrument sounds, explore unique textures, and even generate sound effects that align with their artistic vision. This personalized sonic palette empowers musicians to craft distinctive auditory experiences that resonate with their creative intent.

## Ethical Considerations and Human-AI Collaboration:

While AI assists musicians and composers, ethical considerations come into play. Determining the balance between human intent and AI-generated suggestions is crucial. Additionally, ensuring that AI-generated music respects copyright and avoids plagiarism is a shared responsibility.

## The Creative Future:

The role of AI in assisting musicians and composers marks a profound shift in the creative landscape. This partnership between human imagination and computational ingenuity expands the potential for innovation, pushing the boundaries of musical expression. As AI continues to evolve, musicians and composers stand at the forefront of an artistic renaissance, where technology enhances their creativity and propels the evolution of music into uncharted realms.

## CHAPTER 7
# CHALLENGES AND FUTURE DIRECTIONS

In the dynamic landscape of Artificial Intelligence (AI), the interplay between innovation and challenge defines our trajectory into the future. As AI systems continue to advance in their ability to mimic human cognition and decision-making, we stand at a crucial juncture where we must navigate the complexities and uncertainties that accompany this technological revolution. This chapter invites us to embark on a thoughtful exploration of the challenges and promising directions that lie ahead, offering insights into how we can harness AI's vast potential while addressing the ethical, societal, and technical hurdles that accompany it.

**Unveiling Complexity and Responsibility:**

The rise of AI brings forth a myriad of challenges, some of which are deeply intertwined with the technology's own complexity. The opacity of AI decision-making, often described as a "black box," prompts a call for transparency and interpretability. How do we ensure that AI systems provide clear explanations for their decisions, especially when they are employed in critical domains like healthcare or finance? Additionally, the pervasiveness of bias in AI algorithms, stemming from biased training data, necessitates a vigilant commitment to fairness and ethical development.

As AI gains autonomy in making decisions that affect individuals' lives, the ethical responsibility to prevent discrimination, promote fairness, and respect privacy becomes paramount. This chapter explores these and other challenges in the AI landscape, urging us to foster a responsible and human-centric approach as we shape the future of this transformative technology.

## The biases and limitations of Generative AI

Generative AI, which has made significant strides in generating text, images, and audio, is a testament to the remarkable advancements in artificial intelligence. However, like any powerful tool, it carries its own set of biases and limitations that warrant careful consideration.

## Data Bias and Amplification:

Generative AI often learns from large datasets sourced from the internet, which inherently contain biases present in society. This data bias can manifest as biases in the generated content. For example, language models may generate text that reflects and perpetuates racial, gender, or cultural biases present in their training data. These biases, when amplified by AI, can have real-world consequences, from reinforcing stereotypes to exacerbating societal inequalities.

## Creative Output vs. Human Values:

Generative AI can produce content that may be creative and novel but doesn't necessarily align with human values and ethics. AI-generated art, music, or text may sometimes lack cultural sensitivity or emotional depth, leading to potential misunderstandings or misinterpretations. Balancing the creative output of AI with ethical considerations is an ongoing challenge.

## Lack of Contextual Understanding:

Generative AI often lacks a deep understanding of context. It generates content based on patterns in the training data but may not comprehend the nuances, emotions, or implications of the generated output. This can result in AI generating content that is contextually inappropriate or even offensive.

## Over-optimization and Lack of Diversity:

AI models can sometimes over-optimize during training, leading to the generation of content that closely mimics their training data but lacks diversity and originality. This limitation can result in repetitive or formulaic outputs, hindering the exploration of genuinely novel creative possibilities.

## Ethical and Legal Challenges:

AI-generated content poses ethical and legal challenges. Questions about copyright, ownership, and the authenticity of AI-generated works are still evolving. Determining how to attribute authorship and ownership in AI-generated content is a complex issue that requires legal and ethical frameworks.

## Mitigation and Ethical Development:

Addressing the biases and limitations of Generative AI requires a multi-faceted approach. This includes improving training data to reduce biases, implementing fairness and bias detection tools, and fostering a culture of ethical AI development. It's also crucial to involve diverse voices in AI development to ensure a more comprehensive understanding of cultural nuances and ethical considerations.

## Future Directions:

The future of Generative AI lies in mitigating biases, improving interpretability and transparency, and finding ways to harmonize AI-generated content with human values and creativity. This involves ongoing research, collaboration between AI developers and domain experts, and the responsible use of Generative AI in various applications. By addressing these biases and limitations, we can unlock the full potential of Generative AI while ensuring it aligns with the ethical and societal values we hold dear.

## Overcoming mode collapse and instability in training

Training Generative Adversarial Networks (GANs), which consist of a generator and a discriminator network, can be a challenging endeavor due to issues like mode collapse and training instability. Mode collapse occurs when the generator fails to produce diverse samples, focusing on a limited set of outputs. Training instability can manifest as oscillations or convergence issues in the training process. Overcoming these challenges is crucial for producing high-quality and diverse AI-generated content.

## Understanding Mode Collapse:

Mode collapse happens when the generator produces a limited range of outputs, often failing to explore the full diversity of the target distribution. Instead of generating a wide variety of samples, it settles into a pattern where it repeatedly produces similar or identical outputs. Mode collapse can occur when the discriminator becomes too adept at identifying fake samples, leading the generator to over-optimize for a narrow range of outputs that fool the discriminator.

## Addressing Mode Collapse:

Several strategies can mitigate mode collapse. One approach is to use more complex network architectures for both the generator and discriminator. Another technique is to employ regularization methods like gradient penalties to encourage the generator to explore a broader range of outputs. Additionally, using techniques like minibatch discrimination and feature matching can help stabilize training and reduce mode collapse.

## Training Instability:

GAN training can be inherently unstable. The generator and discriminator networks engage in a dynamic adversarial process where the generator aims to produce realistic samples while the discriminator seeks to distinguish real from fake samples. This tension can lead to oscillations and difficulties in achieving convergence.

**Stabilizing GAN Training:**

Several methods can help stabilize GAN training. One key strategy is progressive training, where the complexity of the network is gradually increased over time. This method starts with simpler tasks before moving to more complex ones, allowing the network to learn progressively. Additionally, using appropriate initialization techniques, batch normalization, and adaptive learning rate schedules can contribute to more stable training.

**Regularization Techniques:**

Regularization methods such as weight clipping and gradient penalties can also improve training stability. These techniques ensure that the discriminator does not become too dominant, allowing the generator to continue exploring the sample space.

**Balancing Act:**

Achieving a balance between the generator and discriminator is crucial for stable GAN training. Ensuring that neither network becomes too dominant is key to preventing training instability and mode collapse.

**Ethical considerations: potential misuse and responsible AI development**

As Artificial Intelligence (AI) continues to advance, it brings to the forefront critical ethical considerations surrounding its potential misuse and the imperative of responsible AI development. The transformative power of AI, capable of impacting diverse domains such as healthcare, finance, autonomous vehicles, and more, necessitates a vigilant commitment to ethical principles that safeguard human well-being, fairness, privacy, and societal values.

## Potential Misuse of AI:

AI, like any powerful tool, can be misused. One concern is the use of AI in surveillance and privacy infringements. Advanced facial recognition technologies, for example, raise concerns about mass surveillance and the erosion of personal privacy. Moreover, AI-driven disinformation campaigns and deepfake technology pose significant threats to truth and trust in an era marked by information warfare.

## Bias and Fairness:

Bias in AI algorithms, often inherited from biased training data, can perpetuate inequalities. In areas like hiring, lending, and criminal justice, biased AI decision-making can lead to discriminatory outcomes. Addressing these biases and ensuring fairness in AI systems is an ethical imperative.

## Accountability and Transparency:

The complexity of AI can make it challenging to determine accountability when AI systems make decisions that impact individuals' lives. It's essential to develop methods that render AI decisions transparent and understandable, allowing individuals to question, challenge, and appeal algorithmic outcomes.

**Responsible AI Development:**

To mitigate these ethical concerns, responsible AI development is paramount. This involves incorporating ethical considerations into every stage of AI system development, from data collection and model training to deployment and ongoing monitoring. It also necessitates interdisciplinary collaboration between AI developers, ethicists, policymakers, and domain experts.

**Ethical Frameworks and Regulations:**

The development of ethical frameworks and regulations is essential for guiding AI development. These frameworks can establish guidelines for the responsible use of AI, ensuring that technology aligns with human values and societal norms. Policymakers play a vital role in creating and enforcing regulations that safeguard against AI misuse.

**Human-Centric AI:**

Ultimately, AI should be designed to augment human capabilities, not replace them. A human-centric approach ensures that AI is developed in ways that enhance human well-being, support decision-making, and respect individual rights and freedoms.

**The Ongoing Journey:**

As AI continues to evolve, ethical considerations must remain at its core. This includes addressing potential misuse, combating bias, enhancing transparency, and fostering a culture of responsible AI development. By prioritizing ethical principles, we can harness the vast potential of AI while safeguarding the values and rights that define our society.

## The future of Generative AI: human-AI collaboration and co-creation

The future of Generative AI is a symphony of human-AI collaboration, where artificial intelligence acts as a creative partner, extending the capabilities and imagination of human creators. This transformative journey into AI-assisted co-creation promises to redefine how we generate art, music, text, and more, leading to innovative and novel expressions that push the boundaries of human creativity.

## Co-Creation in the Arts:

In the realm of the arts, Generative AI offers a canvas where human artists and machines collaborate to craft masterpieces. Musicians can compose with AI-generated accompaniments, painters can use AI to inspire new visual concepts, and writers can find creative sparks in AI-generated text. This collaborative process enriches the creative journey, offering fresh perspectives, imaginative twists, and an expansive repertoire of possibilities.

## Enhancing Creativity:

AI acts as an enabler, enhancing the creative process rather than replacing it. It can suggest novel ideas, provide instant feedback, and help artists explore uncharted territories. For musicians, AI-generated melodies can serve as a starting point for composition, which they can then personalize with their emotional nuances. Visual artists can use AI to generate initial drafts, adding their unique touch to create one-of-akind artworks. This collaboration harnesses the strengths of both humans and AI, resulting in creations that resonate with depth and innovation.

## Innovating in Industry:

Generative AI is not confined to the arts alone. It is revolutionizing industries such as design, architecture, fashion, and content creation. Architects can use AI to generate building designs that optimize energy efficiency, while fashion designers can experiment with AI-generated textile patterns. In content creation, AI can generate video game levels, film scripts, and marketing materials, saving time and providing fresh content ideas.

## Ethical Considerations:

Human-AI collaboration also raises ethical considerations. Ensuring that AI respects copyright, intellectual property rights, and ethical boundaries is crucial. The ownership and attribution of AI-generated works require clear frameworks. Moreover, AI-generated content should align with cultural sensitivity and respect diverse perspectives.

## Education and Skills:

As AI increasingly becomes a creative partner, education and training programs should equip individuals with the skills needed to collaborate effectively with AI. Artists, writers, and creators of all kinds will benefit from understanding how to leverage AI tools while maintaining their artistic integrity.

**A Harmonious Future:**

The future of Generative AI is a harmonious blend of human ingenuity and artificial intelligence, where co-creation drives innovation and artistic expression. This partnership extends beyond what each can achieve in isolation, offering a tantalizing glimpse into a future where the creative boundaries are limitless, and the artistic landscape is enriched by the symphony of human-AI collaboration.

# CHAPTER 8
# CREATIVE WRITING AND STORYTELLING

The evolution of Artificial Intelligence (AI) has ushered in a remarkable era for creative writing and storytelling, where machines become co-authors and sources of boundless inspiration. This chapter embarks on a journey into the world of generative AI for creative writing and storytelling, where algorithms and neural networks collaborate with human authors to craft narratives, poems, and literary worlds that evoke emotions, provoke thought, and challenge the boundaries of human imagination.

The fusion of AI and creative writing is a testament to the ever-expanding boundaries of technology's role in artistry. As AI models gain the capacity to generate text that is coherent, contextually aware, and emotionally resonant, they stand as creative partners in a literary renaissance. This synergy between human storytelling prowess and machine computational abilities has the potential to redefine how we conceive, draft, and experience literature.

Generative AI empowers writers to explore new creative horizons. It can spark ideas, provide alternative perspectives, and even co-create entire narratives. Whether it's generating poetic verses, suggesting plot twists, or assisting in character development, AI's involvement amplifies the creative process, enriching the literary output and challenging conventional notions of authorship.

As we navigate the terrain where technology and imagination converge, we embark on a literary journey that promises to be as innovative as it is imaginative. In the realm of generative AI for creative writing and storytelling, the page becomes a canvas where the lines between human and machine creativity blur, inviting us to rethink the very essence of storytelling and the limitless possibilities of literary expression.

## AI assistance in brainstorming and ideation

Brainstorming and ideation are pivotal stages in the creative process, where innovative ideas take root and flourish. In recent years, Artificial Intelligence (AI) has emerged as a valuable partner in these endeavors, offering tools and techniques that augment human creativity, foster idea generation, and enhance problem-solving. This chapter delves into the ways in which AI assists in brainstorming and ideation, propelling the creative process to new heights.

## Idea Generation:

AI-driven tools can stimulate idea generation by providing a constant flow of suggestions and insights. For example, in the context of creative writing, AI can propose alternative plot twists, character arcs, or story settings, sparking fresh narrative ideas. In design, AI-generated visual concepts can inspire creative directions for graphic artists, architects, and product designers. These AI-generated suggestions often serve as creative prompts, challenging human creators to explore new angles and possibilities.

## Content Recommendations:

AI systems, particularly those built on natural language processing (NLP) and machine learning, excel in content recommendation. They analyze vast datasets to understand user preferences and can suggest relevant ideas, articles, books, or research papers. For content creators, these recommendations serve as valuable sources of inspiration, helping them explore diverse perspectives and accumulate knowledge to fuel their ideation process.

## Data Analysis and Pattern Recognition:

AI's data analysis capabilities are instrumental in identifying patterns and trends that might elude human perception. In fields such as market research, finance, and scientific discovery, AI algorithms can process vast amounts of data, extract meaningful insights, and generate innovative ideas for business strategies, investments, or research projects. By surfacing hidden connections, AI enhances the quality and depth of ideation.

## Collaborative Ideation:

AI-powered collaboration tools facilitate ideation in a collaborative context. Virtual whiteboards equipped with AI features enable teams to brainstorm and visualize ideas in real time, irrespective of geographical boundaries. These tools often incorporate AI-driven ideation techniques, such as mind mapping and concept clustering, to organize thoughts and concepts, fostering collaborative creativity.

## Personalized Ideation:

AI can provide personalized ideation support tailored to an individual's creative preferences and goals. For instance, in music composition, AI can generate chord progressions or melodies that align with a musician's preferred style or mood. In marketing, AI can suggest campaign ideas based on a brand's identity and target audience. This personalized approach augments creativity by aligning AI-generated ideas with individual creative visions.

The integration of AI into brainstorming and ideation opens doors to uncharted creative horizons. It blurs the line between human and machine creativity, fostering a symbiotic relationship where AI acts as both muse and collaborator. As AI continues to advance, it promises to be an indispensable companion on the journey of ideation, expanding the limits of human imagination and innovation.

## Plot generation and character development

The art of storytelling hinges on compelling plots and well-rounded characters, and Artificial Intelligence (AI) has emerged as a valuable tool in shaping these fundamental elements of narrative. Through the application of natural language processing (NLP) and machine learning, AI offers writers, screenwriters, game developers, and creatives of all kinds the ability to generate intricate plots and breathe life into multifaceted characters. This chapter explores the ways in which AI contributes to plot generation and character development, enriching the creative landscape.

## Plot Generation:

AI-driven tools can assist in plot generation by providing creative prompts, suggesting plot twists, or even co-creating entire storylines. For instance, in creative writing, AI can propose alternative narrative directions, helping authors explore diverse story arcs and unexpected developments. In film and television, AI can assist screenwriters in crafting engaging plots by analyzing audience preferences and successful storytelling patterns. These AI-generated ideas serve as sparks that ignite the creative process, inspiring storytellers to craft narratives that resonate with audiences.

## Character Development:

AI's role in character development extends beyond plot generation. It can aid in creating well-defined, multidimensional characters by analyzing character traits, motivations, and arcs. In video game design, AI can assist in generating non-player characters (NPCs) with distinct personalities and behaviors, enhancing the player's immersive experience. For novelists and screenwriters, AI can help create character profiles, ensuring consistency in a character's traits, speech, and actions throughout the narrative.

## Data-Driven Insights:

AI leverages vast datasets to offer data-driven insights into plot and character development. By analyzing existing stories, AI systems identify common narrative structures, character archetypes, and emotional arcs that resonate with audiences. Writers can draw upon these insights to craft narratives that are both innovative and emotionally engaging.

## Personalized Storytelling:

AI has the capacity to personalize storytelling experiences. In interactive media, such as video games or choose-your-own-adventure narratives, AI can adapt the plot and character interactions based on player choices, creating a unique narrative journey for each player. Similarly, in marketing, AI can tailor brand stories and advertisements to individual customer profiles, making the storytelling experience more relevant and engaging.

The future of AI in plot generation and character development is one of collaborative creativity. AI serves as a partner, offering inspiration, insights, and efficiency while respecting the unique creative vision of human authors and storytellers. As AI continues to evolve, it will provide storytellers with new tools and approaches to craft narratives that captivate, inspire, and resonate with audiences worldwide.

## Interactive storytelling with AI

Interactive storytelling, a dynamic form of narrative engagement, has found a powerful ally in Artificial Intelligence (AI). AI-driven interactive storytelling offers audiences personalized and immersive narrative experiences, where their choices and actions influence the plot, characters, and outcomes. In this chapter, we explore the innovative landscape of interactive storytelling with AI, shedding light on the techniques, applications, and ethical considerations that shape this evolving art form.

## Dynamic Narrative Structures:

AI empowers interactive storytelling by enabling dynamic narrative structures. Traditional linear narratives give way to branching storylines, where the audience's decisions dictate the direction of the plot. AI algorithms analyze user choices and seamlessly adapt the narrative, creating a diverse array of story arcs and endings tailored to individual preferences.

## Gaming and Entertainment:

The gaming industry has been a pioneer in embracing AI-powered interactive storytelling. Games use AI to create non-linear narratives, where players' decisions influence the unfolding story. Games like "The Witcher" series offer complex branching narratives with multiple possible endings, providing players with agency over the story's progression.

## Educational and Training Applications:

AI-driven interactive storytelling extends beyond entertainment. In educational and training contexts, interactive narratives serve as powerful tools for engagement and learning. AI can adapt educational content to a learner's pace and preferences, creating personalized learning journeys. In corporate training, interactive scenarios simulate real-world challenges, allowing employees to develop critical skills in a risk-free environment.

## Conversational Agents and Chatbots:

Conversational AI agents and chatbots bring interactivity to storytelling through dialogue. These agents engage users in natural language conversations, guiding them through narrative experiences. In customer service, chatbots can provide interactive narratives to assist users in troubleshooting or navigating complex processes.

## Ethical Considerations:

The use of AI in interactive storytelling introduces ethical considerations. Privacy and data security are paramount, as user interactions are often recorded and analyzed to personalize narratives. There are concerns about AI-generated content aligning with ethical standards, avoiding offensive or biased narratives, and ensuring that AI respects cultural sensitivities.

## The Future of Interactive Storytelling:

The future of interactive storytelling with AI is one of boundless creativity and engagement. As AI algorithms become more sophisticated, they will craft narratives that respond to user emotions, adapt to nuanced choices, and blur the line between reality and fiction. The integration of AI with virtual and augmented reality will further enhance immersive storytelling experiences, enabling users to step into the worlds they help shape.

Interactive storytelling with AI holds the promise of deeply engaging, personalized narratives that captivate and educate, transcending the boundaries of traditional storytelling. As AI continues to evolve, it will serve as an invaluable partner in crafting narratives that resonate with audiences in ways previously unimagined.

## Balancing AI-generated content with human creativity

The integration of Artificial Intelligence (AI) in content generation brings forth both opportunities and challenges, particularly in striking a harmonious balance between AI-generated content and human creativity. This chapter explores the complexities and considerations involved in finding equilibrium between the capabilities of AI and the unique ingenuity of human creators in fields like writing, art, music, and more.

## AI's Role as a Creative Partner:

AI serves as a valuable creative partner, offering efficiency, inspiration, and innovative possibilities. In content creation, it can suggest ideas, automate repetitive tasks, and assist in generating drafts. For instance, in writing, AI can propose plot twists or generate text for marketing campaigns, freeing human writers to focus on more creative aspects. In art, AI can provide design suggestions or generate initial sketches, giving artists a starting point for their creations.

## Enhancing Creativity:

AI augments human creativity by offering fresh perspectives and expanding creative horizons. It can introduce creators to new ideas, styles, or genres they might not have considered. Musicians can experiment with AI-generated chord progressions, writers can explore alternative narrative paths, and designers can generate novel visual concepts. This synergy between AI and human creativity fosters a rich ecosystem of innovation.

## Ethical Considerations:

Balancing AI-generated content with human creativity involves ethical considerations. Questions about authorship, intellectual property, and plagiarism arise when AI plays a significant role in content creation. Determining how to attribute authorship and ownership in AI-generated works requires clear legal and ethical frameworks. Additionally, creators must ensure that AI-generated content aligns with cultural sensitivity and respects diverse perspectives.

## Maintaining Human Essence:

While AI contributes to content creation, preserving the human essence in art, music, writing, and other creative endeavors remains essential. Creators should infuse their unique perspectives, emotions, and storytelling into their work, ensuring that AI serves as a tool to enhance their vision rather than replace it. The human touch, with its depth of emotion and personal experiences, remains irreplaceable.

In this dynamic landscape, creators, technologists, and policymakers must work together to foster an environment where AI enhances human creativity while upholding ethical and artistic values. Striking the right balance between AI and human creativity is an ongoing journey, one that promises to redefine the possibilities of artistic expression in the digital age.

# CHAPTER 9

# INDUSTRY TRANSFORMATIONS

In the ever-evolving landscape of business and technology, the term "industry transformations" has become more than just a catchphrase; it's a dynamic force that reshapes the way we live, work, and interact with the world. The journey of industries from their traditional forms to modern, tech-driven powerhouses is a narrative of innovation, disruption, and adaptation. This section delves into the profound changes that have swept across various sectors, touching upon the pivotal role of emerging technologies, shifts in consumer behavior, and the relentless pursuit of efficiency and sustainability.

**A Revolution Powered by Technology:**

At the heart of industry transformations lies technology, the catalyst that propels sectors forward into uncharted territories. The advent of the internet, mobile devices, big data, and artificial intelligence has revolutionized the way businesses operate. Digitization and automation have rendered traditional processes obsolete, ushering in a new era of efficiency and connectivity. As industries embrace these digital tools, they gain unprecedented insights, streamline operations, and create innovative products and services that resonate with modern consumers.

## Consumer-Centric Evolution:

Consumer behavior, expectations, and preferences have evolved dramatically in tandem with technological advancements. Today's consumers seek personalized experiences, seamless digital interactions, and sustainable solutions. Industries have had to pivot towards customer-centric models, employing data-driven insights to tailor their offerings and engage with their audiences on a deeper level. This shift places the consumer at the center of decision-making, driving the creation of products and services that meet their ever-changing needs.

## Globalization and Collaboration:

The interconnectedness of our world through globalization has redefined industry boundaries. Businesses no longer operate in isolation; they are part of complex global ecosystems. Partnerships, collaborations, and supply chain networks span continents, enabling the flow of goods, services, and ideas at an unprecedented scale. Industry transformations often hinge on the ability of organizations to navigate this interconnected web, leveraging the strengths of diverse players to drive innovation and growth.

**Sustainability and Responsibility:**

As industries evolve, sustainability and corporate responsibility have emerged as critical imperatives. Climate change, resource depletion, and social concerns demand that businesses operate with an eye toward long-term sustainability. Industry leaders are not only adopting eco-friendly practices but are also driving innovation in clean energy, circular economies, and socially responsible business models.

**Challenges and Opportunities:**

While industry transformations present boundless opportunities for growth and innovation, they are not without challenges. Legacy systems, resistance to change, and the need for upskilling the workforce can pose hurdles on the path to transformation. Additionally, ethical considerations, data privacy, and cybersecurity remain pressing concerns in the digital age.

**Navigating the Future:**

In this exploration of industry transformations, we delve into specific sectors, examining how they have evolved, adapted, and innovated in response to the forces of change. From finance to healthcare, manufacturing to entertainment, each industry tells a unique story of resilience and reinvention. The lessons learned along the way serve as beacons for organizations embarking on their own transformation journeys, guiding them towards a future where they are not just participants in industries but architects of their evolution.

In the chapters that follow, we embark on a journey through these industry transformations, uncovering the technologies, trends, and strategies that have shaped the present and will define the future. We invite you to explore the remarkable tapestry of change that is reshaping our world, one industry at a time.

## Generative AI in fashion: designing, styling, and virtual try-ons

The fashion industry is no stranger to innovation and creativity, but in recent years, it has witnessed a transformative shift with the integration of generative AI. This technological revolution has permeated every aspect of the fashion lifecycle, from design and styling to virtual try-ons. Here, we delve into how generative AI is redefining the fashion industry and shaping the way we dress and shop.

## Design and Creativity:

Generative AI has empowered fashion designers with a novel source of inspiration. By analyzing vast datasets of historical fashion trends, AI algorithms can generate design concepts that blend traditional styles with cutting-edge innovation. Designers can collaborate with AI, using its creative suggestions as a springboard to craft unique, trendsetting collections.

## Pattern Generation and Customization:

Creating intricate patterns and textures is a labor-intensive process in fashion design. Generative AI simplifies this task by generating patterns automatically. Moreover, it enables customization at scale, allowing consumers to personalize their clothing with unique patterns, colors, and styles.

**Styling Recommendations:**

Online fashion retailers are leveraging generative AI to enhance the shopping experience. AI-driven styling recommendations take into account individual preferences, body types, and current fashion trends, helping customers assemble outfits that suit their taste and occasion. This personalization enhances customer satisfaction and boosts sales.

**Virtual Try-Ons and Augmented Reality:**

Virtual try-ons have revolutionized online shopping. Generative AI, combined with augmented reality (AR), enables customers to virtually try on clothing and accessories from the comfort of their homes. AI algorithms accurately map clothing onto a customer's body, providing a realistic preview of how an outfit will look and fit.

**Supply Chain Optimization:**

Fashion brands are optimizing their supply chains with generative AI. Predictive modeling helps forecast demand more accurately, reducing overproduction and waste. AI also aids in inventory management, ensuring that the right products are available at the right time.

**Sustainable Fashion:**

Sustainability is a growing concern in the fashion industry. Generative AI plays a role in designing sustainable clothing by optimizing material usage, reducing waste, and finding eco-friendly alternatives. AI-driven supply chain management also minimizes the environmental impact of production and distribution.

## Creative Collaborations:

AI is becoming a creative collaborator in fashion photography and advertising. It can suggest compelling visual concepts, edit images, and even generate marketing copy. This streamlines content creation, making it faster and more cost-effective.

## Predictive Trends:

Generative AI can analyze vast amounts of fashion-related data, such as social media posts, runway shows, and retail sales. By identifying patterns and trends, AI can predict upcoming fashion trends, helping brands stay ahead of the curve in design and marketing.

## Ethical Considerations:

While generative AI offers numerous benefits to the fashion industry, it also raises ethical questions. Issues related to data privacy, algorithmic bias, and the displacement of human jobs in design and retail require careful consideration.

## Personalized marketing through AI-generated content

In the fast-paced world of digital marketing, personalization has become the key to engaging customers and driving conversions. AI-generated content is at the forefront of this transformation, enabling brands to deliver highly tailored and relevant messages to their audiences. In this section, we explore how AI is revolutionizing personalized marketing strategies, from dynamic product recommendations to individualized email campaigns.

## Understanding Customer Behavior:

AI-powered marketing begins with data. Machine learning algorithms analyze vast amounts of customer data, including browsing history, purchase behavior, and social media interactions. This analysis provides valuable insights into customer preferences and behavior patterns.

## Segmenting Audiences:

AI allows marketers to segment their audiences into highly specific groups based on shared characteristics and behaviors. These segments can be as broad as demographics or as granular as individual customer profiles. This segmentation is the foundation of personalized marketing campaigns.

## Personalized Product Recommendations:

One of the most recognizable applications of AI in marketing is personalized product recommendations. By analyzing a customer's past purchases and behavior, AI algorithms can suggest products that align with their interests and preferences. This increases the likelihood of upselling and cross-selling.

## Dynamic Content Generation:

AI can generate dynamic content for websites, emails, and ads in real-time. For example, a clothing retailer can display different product recommendations and promotions to individual customers based on their browsing history and preferences. This level of personalization enhances the user experience and conversion rates.

## Email Personalization:

Personalized email marketing goes beyond addressing recipients by their first name. AI can craft entire email campaigns tailored to each recipient's interests and behavior. From subject lines to product recommendations and content, every element is optimized for maximum engagement.

## Predictive Analytics:

AI-powered predictive analytics can forecast customer behavior, such as the likelihood of making a purchase or churning. Marketers can use these insights to proactively engage with customers, offering discounts or incentives to retain their business.

## Chatbots and Virtual Assistants:

AI-driven chatbots and virtual assistants provide personalized customer support and recommendations in real-time. They can answer questions, guide customers through the purchasing process, and suggest relevant products or services.

## Personalization at Scale:

AI enables personalized marketing at scale. Even as the customer base grows, AI algorithms can continue to deliver individualized experiences. This scalability is essential for e-commerce platforms and global brands with diverse audiences.

## Ethical Considerations:

As with any AI application, there are ethical considerations in personalized marketing. Privacy concerns, data security, and algorithmic bias must be addressed to ensure that personalization efforts respect customer rights and do not inadvertently discriminate.

## Impact on entertainment: AI-generated scripts and special effects

The entertainment industry, including film, television, and gaming, has long been a bastion of creativity and innovation. With the integration of AI, this creative landscape is undergoing a profound transformation. AI is now contributing to the creation of scripts, characters, and even special effects, redefining storytelling and visual experiences in entertainment.

## AI-Generated Scripts:

***Scriptwriting Assistance:*** AI algorithms analyze vast datasets of existing scripts, movies, and genres to assist screenwriters in developing compelling narratives. They can provide suggestions for plot twists, dialogue, and character development.

***Genre Exploration:*** AI can generate scripts in various genres, from romantic comedies to sci-fi thrillers, helping writers and studios explore new creative territories and tap into diverse audience interests.

***Content Adaptation:*** AI can adapt existing content into scripts, making it easier to create adaptations, remakes, or spin-offs of popular films and series.

## Character Creation:

***Character Development:*** AI-driven tools help writers and designers create well-rounded characters by suggesting backstories, motivations, and personality traits based on predefined criteria.

***Virtual Actors:*** AI can generate digital avatars or virtual actors that can be used in films, animations, and video games, reducing the need for physical actors and offering new possibilities for storytelling.

## Special Effects and CGI:

***Enhanced Visual Effects:*** AI-enhanced CGI (Computer-Generated Imagery) improves the quality and realism of visual effects in films and games. AI algorithms can generate lifelike simulations of natural phenomena, creatures, and environments.

***Facial Animation:*** AI can analyze real-world facial expressions and movements to create highly realistic facial animations for characters in animations and games.

***Automated Animation:*** AI automates animation processes, making it more cost-effective and efficient for studios. Motion capture combined with AI can generate complex character animations.

## Content Personalization:

***Tailored Content:*** AI-driven recommendation systems personalize content recommendations for viewers based on their preferences and viewing history, enhancing the streaming experience.

## Post-Production Assistance:

***Video Editing:*** AI-powered video editing tools can automatically cut, edit, and compile footage, saving time and resources in post-production.

***Sound Design:*** AI analyzes audio data to generate custom sound effects, music, and even voiceovers for films, games, and animations.

## Predictive Analytics:

***Audience Insights:*** AI-driven analytics provide studios and content creators with insights into audience preferences and trends, helping them make data-informed decisions about content creation and distribution.

## Ethical Considerations:

The use of AI in entertainment raises ethical concerns, particularly in areas like deepfakes and bias in character creation. Ensuring ethical use of AI in entertainment, respecting copyrights, and addressing concerns about manipulated content is crucial.

## Innovations in product design and architecture

Product design and architecture are two fields where innovation has always been at the forefront. In recent years, the integration of advanced technologies and novel approaches has brought about transformative changes, redefining how products are conceived, developed, and built, as well as how buildings are designed and constructed.

## 1. Product Design:

*Digital Prototyping:* Product design has evolved with the use of digital prototyping. 3D modeling and simulation tools allow designers to create and test prototypes digitally, reducing the need for physical prototypes, which can be time-consuming and expensive.

*Generative Design:* AI-driven generative design tools assist designers in exploring a wide range of design options. These algorithms consider various parameters, such as materials and manufacturing constraints, to generate optimal designs.

*Additive Manufacturing (3D Printing):* 3D printing technology has revolutionized product design. It allows for the creation of complex and customized products that were previously difficult or impossible to manufacture using traditional methods.

*Sustainability Integration:* Sustainability is a critical consideration in product design. Innovations include designing products for recyclability, using eco-friendly materials, and employing life cycle analysis to reduce environmental impact.

*Human-Centered Design:* Human-centered design principles emphasize creating products that prioritize user experience and accessibility, leading to more inclusive and user-friendly designs.


## 2. Architecture:

***Parametric Design:*** Parametric design, often aided by computational tools, enables architects to create complex, variable, and highly customized structures. It is particularly useful in designing buildings with intricate geometries.

***BIM (Building Information Modeling):*** BIM is a digital representation of a building's physical and functional characteristics. It streamlines the design and construction process by facilitating collaboration among architects, engineers, and contractors.

***Sustainable Architecture:*** Sustainable architecture incorporates environmentally friendly features such as green roofs, energy-efficient systems, and passive design strategies to reduce energy consumption and minimize environmental impact.

***Smart Buildings:*** Smart building technology integrates IoT (Internet of Things) sensors and systems to enhance the functionality and efficiency of buildings. This includes energy management, security, and occupant comfort.

***Prefab and Modular Construction:*** Prefabrication and modular construction methods have gained traction in recent years. They enable faster, more cost-effective, and sustainable building processes.


## 3. Cross-Disciplinary Collaboration:

Collaboration between product designers, architects, engineers, and technologists is becoming increasingly essential. Cross-disciplinary teams leverage diverse expertise to create innovative solutions.

## 4. Virtual Reality (VR) and Augmented Reality (AR):

VR and AR are transforming both product design and architectural visualization. Designers and architects can use VR for immersive walkthroughs, while AR can overlay digital information onto physical spaces.

## 5. Ethical and Sustainable Design:

Ethical considerations in design and architecture include addressing social and environmental impacts, such as ensuring accessibility for all and reducing carbon footprints.

## 6. Computational Tools and AI:

Computational design tools and AI are automating complex design tasks, enabling architects and designers to explore more design options and optimize for various criteria.

# CHAPTER 10

# BUILDING YOUR OWN GENERATIVE AI

In an era where artificial intelligence (AI) stands as one of the most transformative technologies, the journey of exploration and innovation beckons to those who seek to craft their own generative AI systems. This chapter ventures into the exciting realm of building your own generative AI, where curiosity and creativity converge to shape the future of AI-driven possibilities. Here, we embark on a journey that empowers you to design, develop, and deploy AI systems that generate text, images, music, and more, placing the tools of generative AI at your fingertips.

**A World of Creative Potential:**

Generative AI opens the door to a world of creative potential, where algorithms and neural networks become your canvas for artistic expression and problem-solving. Whether you aspire to create AI-generated art, craft compelling stories, or generate music that stirs the soul, building your own generative AI empowers you to infuse your unique vision into AI-driven creations. This journey is not limited to artists and writers alone; it welcomes innovators, scientists, and entrepreneurs who see AI as a means to revolutionize industries and push the boundaries of what is possible.

## The Power of DIY AI:

Building your own generative AI is a journey of discovery and innovation. It allows you to understand the inner workings of AI systems, experiment with cutting-edge technologies, and tailor AI models to your specific needs. Moreover, it provides a platform for ethical and responsible AI development, where you have the agency to ensure that AI-generated content aligns with your values and intentions.

## An Ethical and Responsible Path:

As you embark on the path of building generative AI, ethical considerations remain paramount. Ensuring that your AI models respect privacy, avoid biases, and adhere to ethical guidelines is not just a choice but a responsibility. This chapter guides you on the ethical dimensions of AI development, helping you navigate the complex terrain of responsible AI creation.

## The Adventure Begins:

The adventure of building your own generative AI is a thrilling odyssey into the heart of AI innovation. It invites you to unleash your imagination, explore the limitless possibilities of AI-driven creativity, and contribute to the ever-expanding landscape of artificial intelligence. As we delve into the intricacies of DIY AI development, you will discover that the journey itself is as rewarding as the AI creations you bring to life.

## Introduction to tools and frameworks

The world of generative AI is teeming with innovation, but it's the tools and frameworks that form the bedrock of creative exploration and development. In this chapter, we embark on a journey into the realm of tools and frameworks for generative AI, where technology becomes the brushstroke of creativity and the engine of innovation.

## Empowering Creativity:

Generative AI tools and frameworks empower creators, artists, developers, and researchers to bring their ideas to life. These tools are designed to harness the capabilities of AI models, making them accessible and usable, even to those without extensive machine learning expertise. Whether you're an artist seeking to generate AI-driven art, a writer looking for text generation, or a scientist exploring data analysis, these tools serve as your creative arsenal.

## The Landscape of Possibilities:

Generative AI tools and frameworks span a diverse landscape, each tailored to specific creative domains. From the GANs (Generative Adversarial Networks) that generate images to the text generation prowess of language models like GPT (Generative Pre-trained Transformer), the possibilities are vast. In addition, frameworks like TensorFlow and PyTorch provide the underlying structure to develop custom generative AI solutions. This chapter introduces you to this rich ecosystem, helping you navigate the tools that align with your creative aspirations.


## A Path to Innovation:

For those eager to explore, these tools and frameworks are not just a means to an end; they're a pathway to innovation. By leveraging existing models and building upon them, you can craft new AI-driven experiences, whether it's generating art that transcends convention, composing music that resonates with the soul, or creating AI-driven applications that enhance efficiency and insight.


## Ethical and Responsible Development:

As we delve into the world of tools and frameworks, ethical considerations accompany us on this journey. It's crucial to ensure that AI-generated content respects privacy, avoids biases, and aligns with ethical guidelines. These tools offer you the opportunity to shape AI development responsibly, safeguarding the values that matter to you.


## The Adventure Begins:

The exploration of generative AI tools and frameworks is an adventure waiting to unfold. It's a journey into the fusion of human creativity and technological innovation, a voyage where you wield the power to create, innovate, and redefine the boundaries of what's possible. As you delve into the intricacies of these tools, you'll find that the true magic lies not just in the technology itself but in the creative wonders you bring to life with it.

**A step-by-step guide to creating a basic generative model**

Creating a generative model is an exciting journey into the world of artificial intelligence and creativity. Whether you're interested in generating art, text, or any other form of content, this step-by-step guide will walk you through the process of building a basic generative model. It assumes you have some familiarity with programming and machine learning concepts.

## Step 1: Define Your Objective

Begin by clarifying your goal. What type of content do you want to generate? Is it text, images, music, or something else? Define the scope of your project and what you aim to achieve with your generative model.

## Step 2: Gather and Prepare Data

Data is the fuel for generative models. Collect a dataset that aligns with your objective. If you're generating text, you might need a corpus of text documents. For image generation, gather a collection of images. Ensure your data is clean, well-organized, and relevant to your project.

## Step 3: Choose a Generative Model Architecture

Select a generative model architecture that suits your project. For text generation, you can start with recurrent neural networks (RNNs) or transformer-based models. For image generation, consider using generative adversarial networks (GANs) or autoencoders. The choice of architecture depends on your project's specific requirements.

## Step 4: Preprocess Data

Prepare your data for training. This involves tasks like tokenization for text data or resizing and normalizing for images. Data preprocessing is essential for feeding clean and structured data to your generative model.

## Step 5: Build and Train Your Model

Use a deep learning framework like TensorFlow or PyTorch to build your generative model. Define the architecture, specify hyperparameters, and train the model using your preprocessed data. Training times can vary widely based on the complexity of your model and the size of your dataset.

## Step 6: Fine-Tune and Optimize

Iterate on your model. Fine-tune hyperparameters, experiment with different architectures, and optimize your training process. This step may involve several training cycles to achieve the desired results.

## Step 7: Generate Content

Once your generative model is trained and fine-tuned, you can start generating content. Provide a seed or input, and let your model generate text, images, or other forms of content. Experiment with different inputs to explore the diversity of generated output.

## Step 8: Evaluate and Refine

Evaluate the quality of the generated content. Does it meet your project's objectives? Use metrics and human evaluation to assess the performance of your generative model. Refine your model based on the feedback and insights gained during this evaluation.

## Step 9: Deploy and Integrate

If your goal is to deploy your generative model for real-world use, integrate it into your application or platform. Ensure that it operates efficiently and reliably in the production environment.

## Step 10: Maintain and Improve

Generative models require ongoing maintenance and improvement. Monitor their performance, collect user feedback, and continue to refine your model to enhance its capabilities.

Remember that creating generative models is an iterative process, and the quality of output improves with time and effort. Don't be discouraged by initial results, and keep experimenting to achieve the creative and technical outcomes you desire. Enjoy the journey of exploring the limitless possibilities of generative AI.

## How to implement Generative AI

Creating a Generative AI system involves several steps, and the specific implementation can vary depending on your goals and the type of generative model you want to build. However, I can provide you with a general step-by-step guide for implementing a basic Generative AI using a deep learning framework like TensorFlow or PyTorch. In this example, we'll focus on building a simple Generative

Adversarial Network (GAN) for generating images. GANs consist of a generator and a discriminator network, which compete against each other to improve the quality of generated content.

## Step 1: Set Up Your Environment

Before you start coding, make sure you have Python, a deep learning framework (e.g., TensorFlow or PyTorch), and any necessary libraries installed. You may also want to use a GPU for faster training.

Setting up your programming environment for Generative AI involves installing the necessary software, libraries, and tools. Below, I'll provide a step-by-step guide for setting up a Python environment for Generative AI using TensorFlow as an example.

## Install Python

If you don't already have Python installed on your system, download and install it from the official website: https://www.python.org/downloads/

## Create a Virtual Environment (Optional but Recommended)

Using a virtual environment helps you keep your project dependencies isolated. Open a terminal/command prompt and run the following commands:

```
# Install the virtualenv package (if not already installed)
pip install virtualenv

# Create a new virtual environment (replace 'myenv' with your
preferred environment name)

virtualenv myenv

# Activate the virtual environment

# On Windows:

Myenv/Scripts/activate
# On macOS and Linux:

source myenv/bin/activate
```

## Install Required Packages

You'll need several libraries and frameworks for Generative AI, with TensorFlow being a popular choice. Install the required packages within your virtual environment:

```
pip install tensorflow

# Install TensorFlow

pip install numpy

# NumPy for numerical operations

pip install matplotlib

# Matplotlib for data visualization (optional)

pip install jupyterlab

# Jupyter Lab for interactive coding (optional)
```

## GPU Support (Optional but Recommended)

If you have an NVIDIA GPU, you can accelerate your deep learning training significantly by installing GPU support for TensorFlow. To do this, you need to install the GPU version of TensorFlow, along with the appropriate CUDA and cuDNN libraries.

```
pip install tensorflow-gpu
```

Ensure that you have compatible versions of CUDA and cuDNN installed. Refer to the TensorFlow documentation for the specific versions required.

## Test Your Setup

To verify that everything is set up correctly, you can create a simple Python script that imports TensorFlow and checks if it runs without errors:

```python
import tensorflow as tf
# Check TensorFlow version and GPU availability
print("TensorFlow version:", tf.__version__)
print("GPU available:",
tf.config.list_physical_devices('GPU'))
# Test if TensorFlow can see your GPU
tf.test.gpu_device_name()
```

Save this script as test_tensorflow.py and run it using Python:

```
python test_tensorflow.py
```

If everything is set up correctly, you should see the TensorFlow version and GPU availability information.

## IDE or Text Editor (Optional)

Choose an Integrated Development Environment (IDE) or text editor for coding. Some popular choices include PyCharm, Visual Studio Code, Jupyter Lab, or plain text editors like Sublime Text or Atom.

With these steps completed, you have a fully functional Python environment ready for developing Generative AI models using TensorFlow or any other deep learning framework of your choice. Remember to activate your virtual environment whenever you work on your Generative AI projects to ensure a clean and isolated environment.

## Step 2: Define Your Dataset

Choose a dataset that your generative model will learn from. In the case of image generation, you might use datasets like CIFAR-10, MNIST, or your custom dataset.

Defining your dataset is a crucial step in creating a Generative AI model, as it directly impacts the quality and diversity of the content your model can generate. In this section, I'll guide you through the process of preparing and defining your dataset programmatically.

## Data Collection

Start by collecting the data you want to use for training your Generative AI model. The source of your data can vary widely depending on your project's goals. You can collect your dataset from the web, use publicly available datasets, or even create your own data through data collection tools.

Here's an example of how to collect image data using Python and a library like requests for web scraping:

```python
import requests

from PIL import Image

from io import BytesIO

# Example: Collect images from a website

url = "https://example.com/images/"

response = requests.get(url)

html_content = response.text

# Parse HTML content to extract image URLs (use a library like BeautifulSoup)

# Download and save images to a local directory
```

## Data Preprocessing

Once you have your data, you need to preprocess it to ensure it's in a suitable format for training. Data preprocessing steps depend on the nature of your data, but common preprocessing tasks include:

- Resizing images to a consistent resolution.

- Normalizing pixel values to a specific range (e.g., [0, 1] or [-1, 1]).

- Augmenting the data with transformations (e.g., rotations, flips) to increase dataset diversity.

- Encoding categorical data (e.g., one-hot encoding for labels).

Here's an example of resizing and normalizing image data using the Python library PIL (Pillow):

```python
from PIL import Image
# Open and preprocess an image
img = Image.open("image.jpg")
img = img.resize((64, 64))
# Resize to a common resolution
img = img.convert("RGB")
# Ensure it's in RGB format
img = img / 255.0
# Normalize pixel values to [0, 1]
```

## Data Splitting

It's essential to split your dataset into training, validation, and testing subsets to evaluate your model's performance properly. Common splits include 70-80% for training, 10-15% for validation, and 10-15% for testing.

You can use libraries like scikit-learn to perform random splitting:

```python
from sklearn.model_selection import train_test_split
# Split data into training, validation, and testing sets
X_train, X_temp, y_train, y_temp = train_test_split(data, labels, test_size=0.3, random_state=42)
X_val, X_test, y_val, y_test = train_test_split(X_temp,
```

```
y_temp, test_size=0.5, random_state=42)
```

## Data Loading

To efficiently feed your dataset into your Generative AI model, create data loaders that batch and shuffle your data. Libraries like TensorFlow's tf.data or PyTorch's DataLoader are commonly used for this purpose.

Here's a simplified example using TensorFlow:

```
import tensorflow as tf
# Create a TensorFlow dataset
Dataset = tf.data.Dataset.from_tensor_slices( ( X_train, y_train ) )
# Batch, shuffle, and prefetch the dataset
batch_size = 32
dataset = dataset.shuffle( buffer_size=len( X_train ) ).batch(batch_size).prefetch(buffer_size=tf.data.experimental.AUTOTUNE )
```

## Data Exploration and Visualization

Before training your Generative AI model, it's a good practice to explore and visualize your dataset to understand its characteristics and ensure data quality. You can use libraries like matplotlib to create data visualizations.

Here's an example of visualizing images from your dataset:

```
import matplotlib.pyplot as plt
# Visualize some images from the dataset
```

```
plt.figure( figsize = ( 10, 10 ) )
for i in range( 9 ):
    plt.subplot( 3, 3, i + 1 )
    plt.imshow( X_train[i] )
    plt.title( y_train[i] )
    plt.axis( "off" )
plt.show()
```

By following these steps, you'll have a well-defined and preprocessed dataset ready for training your Generative AI model. The choice of dataset and how you preprocess it depends on your specific project and goals, so adapt these steps accordingly.

## Step 3: Build the Generator

Create a generator neural network. This network takes random noise as input and generates data samples that resemble the training data. The architecture typically consists of convolutional layers (in the case of images) followed by transposed convolutional layers to upscale the data.

Building the generator is a critical step when creating a Generative Adversarial Network (GAN) or any generative model. The generator network takes random noise as input and produces data that should resemble the target data you want to generate. Here, we'll walk through the process of building the generator programmatically using Python and TensorFlow as an example.

Import Libraries

First, make sure you have TensorFlow installed, as we'll be using it to build the generator. Import the necessary libraries:

```
import tensorflow as tf

from tensorflow import keras
```

## Define the Generator Model

A typical generator architecture consists of transposed convolutional layers (also known as deconvolutional layers) to upscale the input noise into a higher-dimensional space that resembles your target data. Each layer usually includes batch normalization and a ReLU activation function.

Here's an example of how to define a simple generator model in TensorFlow:

```
def build_generator(input_shape, output_shape):
    model = keras.Sequential()
    # Input layer
    model.add( keras.layers.Input( shape = input_shape ) )
    # Hidden layers
    model.add( keras.layers.Dense( 256, activation='relu' ) )
    model.add( keras.layers.BatchNormalization() )
    model.add( keras.layers.Dense( 512, activation='relu') )
    model.add( keras.layers.BatchNormalization() )
    # Output layer
    model.add( keras.layers.Dense( output_shape, activation='sigmoid') )

    return model
```

In this example, input_shape should match the dimensionality of your input noise, and output_shape should match the dimensionality of the data you want to generate. Adjust the architecture according to your specific problem and data.

## Compile the Generator (Optional)

For some generative models, you may want to compile the generator with an optimizer and a loss function, especially when you're training the generator separately. However, in the context of a GAN, the generator's loss is usually computed indirectly through the GAN's training process, so you can skip this step for now.

## Model Summary

Before using the generator, it's a good practice to print a summary of the model to check its architecture and the number of trainable parameters:

```
generator=build_generator(input_shape=(100,),
output_shape=(64, 64, 3))  # Example input and output shapes
generator.summary()
```

## Generate Fake Data

To generate fake data using your trained generator, you can simply pass random noise as input to the generator:

```
import numpy as np


# Generate random noise
noise = np.random.rand(1, 100)  # Adjust the shape based on
```

```
your generator's input_shape

# Generate fake data
fake_data = generator.predict(noise)
```

Make sure the shape of the noise array matches the input shape of your generator.

**Train the Generator (in the context of a GAN)**

In the context of a GAN, the generator is typically trained along with the discriminator in an adversarial manner. Training details would be provided in the "Training Loop" section at **Step 6**, as it involves interactions with the discriminator.

By following these steps, you can build a basic generator for your Generative AI model using TensorFlow. Remember to adjust the architecture and hyperparameters based on your specific project and dataset.

**Step 4: Build the Discriminator**

Create a discriminator neural network. This network's job is to distinguish between real data from your dataset and fake data generated by the generator. Like the generator, it can also consist of convolutional layers.

Building the discriminator is another critical step in creating a Generative Adversarial Network (GAN) or any generative model. The discriminator network's job is to distinguish between real data from your dataset and fake data generated by the generator. Below, I'll guide you through the process of building the discriminator programmatically using Python and TensorFlow as an example.

## Import Libraries

Ensure you have TensorFlow installed, as we'll be using it to build the discriminator. Import the necessary libraries:

```python
import tensorflow as tf

from tensorflow import keras
```

## Define the Discriminator Model

The discriminator typically consists of convolutional layers, followed by fully connected layers. It takes an input that represents an image (real or fake) and produces a single output value, which can be interpreted as the probability that the input is real (close to 1) or fake (close to 0).

Here's an example of how to define a simple discriminator model in TensorFlow:

```python
def build_discriminator(input_shape):
    model = keras.Sequential()


    # Input layer
    model.add(keras.layers.Input(shape=input_shape))


    # Convolutional layers
    model.add(keras.layers.Conv2D(64, (3, 3), padding='same',
```

```
activation='relu'))

    model.add(keras.layers.MaxPooling2D(pool_size=(2, 2)))


    model.add(keras.layers.Conv2D(128, (3, 3), padding='same',
activation='relu'))
    model.add(keras.layers.MaxPooling2D(pool_size=(2, 2)))


    # Flatten and add fully connected layers
    model.add(keras.layers.Flatten())
    model.add(keras.layers.Dense(128, activation='relu'))


    # Output layer (1 neuron, sigmoid activation)
    model.add(keras.layers.Dense(1, activation='sigmoid'))


    return model
```

In this example, input_shape should match the shape of the data you're using (e.g., (64, 64, 3) for 64x64 color images). You can adjust the architecture, including the number of layers and filters, based on the complexity of your problem and data.

## Compile the Discriminator

Compile the discriminator with an optimizer and a loss function. Since the discriminator aims to classify data as real or fake, a binary cross-entropy loss is commonly used:

```
def compile_discriminator(discriminator):


discriminator.compile(optimizer=keras.optimizers.Adam(lr=0.
```

```
0002, beta_1=0.5),

              loss='binary_crossentropy',

              metrics=['accuracy'])
```

Adjust the learning rate (lr) and other hyperparameters as needed.

## Model Summary

Print a summary of the discriminator model to inspect its architecture and the number of trainable parameters:

```
discriminator = build_discriminator(input_shape=(64, 64, 3))
# Example input shape

discriminator.summary()
```

## Train the Discriminator (in the context of a GAN)

In the context of a GAN, the discriminator is trained to distinguish between real and fake data. You'll train it alongside the generator in an adversarial manner. Training details are provided in the "Training Loop" section as it involves interactions with the generator.

## Evaluate the Discriminator (Optional)

After training, you can evaluate the discriminator's performance by testing it on real and fake data. A well-trained discriminator should have a high accuracy in classifying real and fake data.

## Step 5: Define Loss Functions

For a GAN, you need two loss functions: one for the generator and one for the discriminator. Common choices are the binary cross-entropy loss or Wasserstein loss, depending on the type of GAN you are implementing.

Defining loss functions is a crucial step in training a Generative Adversarial Network (GAN) or any generative model. In a GAN, you have two primary loss functions: one for the generator and one for the discriminator. Below, I'll guide you through the process of defining these loss functions programmatically using Python and TensorFlow as an example.

## Discriminator Loss Function:

The discriminator's loss function measures how well it can distinguish between real and fake data. A common choice for the discriminator's loss function in a binary classification setting is binary cross-entropy loss. This loss penalizes the discriminator based on how well it classifies real and fake samples.

Here's how to define the discriminator's loss function:

```python
import tensorflow as tf

def discriminator_loss(real_output, fake_output):

    real_loss = tf.keras.losses.binary_crossentropy( tf.ones_like( real_output ), real_output )

    fake_loss = tf.keras.losses.binary_crossentropy( tf.zeros_like( fake_output )
```

```
, fake_output )

total_loss = real_loss + fake_loss

return total_loss
```

In this example, real_output and fake_output are the discriminator's predictions for real and fake data, respectively.


## Generator Loss Function:

The generator's loss function measures how well it can generate fake data that resembles real data. In a GAN, the generator's loss is often the negative of the discriminator's loss on the fake data. The generator wants to minimize this loss to create data that is more convincing to the discriminator.

Here's how to define the generator's loss function:

```
def generator_loss(fake_output):
 Return
tf.keras.losses.binary_crossentropy( tf.ones_like( fake_output ),
fake_output )
```

In this example, fake_output represents the discriminator's predictions for the fake data generated by the generator.


## Additional Loss Functions (Optional):

Depending on your specific application and goals, you might also incorporate other loss functions, such as:

**Feature Matching:** It measures the difference between the feature representations of real and generated data at intermediate layers of the discriminator. This encourages the generator to produce data that matches the statistics of the real data at various levels of abstraction.

**Regularization Losses:** L1 or L2 regularization terms can be added to the generator and discriminator losses to prevent overfitting and promote smoother outputs.

## Compile the Discriminator and Generator (in the context of a GAN):

In a GAN, you compile both the discriminator and the generator models separately. The discriminator is compiled with its loss function, while the generator is compiled with its loss function.

```
discriminator.compile(optimizer=discriminator_optimizer,
loss=discriminator_loss)

generator.compile(optimizer=generator_optimizer,
loss=generator_loss)
```

## Additional Loss Considerations (Optional):

Depending on the specific variant of GAN you're implementing and the complexity of your model, you might need to adjust loss functions and incorporate advanced techniques like Wasserstein loss for WGANs or perceptual loss for improving image quality.

These are the fundamental steps for defining loss functions in a GAN. Keep in mind that the choice of loss functions and their parameters can significantly impact the training and performance of your Generative AI model, so it's essential to experiment and fine-tune them based on your project requirements

## Step 6: Training Loop

Train your GAN in a loop where the generator and discriminator are updated alternately. The generator aims to minimize its loss, making the generated data more convincing, while the discriminator aims to maximize its loss, getting better at distinguishing real from fake data.

Here's a simplified training loop:

```
for epoch in range(num_epochs):

  for batch in dataset:

    # Train discriminator

    real_data = batch

    fake_data = generator.generate_fake_data()

 discriminator_loss = compute_discriminator_loss( real_data,
fake_data )

    update_discriminator(discriminator_loss)


    # Train generator

    fake_data = generator.generate_fake_data()

    generator_loss = compute_generator_loss(fake_data)

    update_generator(generator_loss)
```

## Step 7: Generate New Data

Once your GAN is trained, you can use the generator to create new data samples. Provide random noise as input to the generator and obtain generated data.

## Step 8: Evaluate and Fine-Tune

Evaluate the quality of the generated data using metrics and visual inspection. You may need to fine-tune your model's hyperparameters and architecture to achieve better results.

## Step 9: Save and Deploy

Save your trained model and deploy it for generating new content as needed.

Keep in mind that this is a simplified overview of the steps involved in implementing a Generative AI model. Depending on your specific project, you may need to dive deeper into various techniques and considerations, such as normalization, regularization, and advanced GAN variants like DCGANs, WGANs, or conditional GANs. Additionally, working with real-world datasets may require data preprocessing and augmentation.

# CHAPTER 11
# ETHICAL CONSIDERATIONS AND SOCIETAL IMPACT

In the ever-evolving landscape of artificial intelligence, the emergence of generative AI has heralded a new era of creativity, innovation, and transformative potential. Generative AI, capable of crafting art, composing music, and generating content autonomously, wields the power to reshape industries, redefine human creativity, and reimagine the boundaries of what machines can achieve. Yet, as this remarkable technology unlocks the door to unprecedented creative horizons, it simultaneously raises a host of profound ethical considerations and exerts far-reaching societal impacts that demand careful exploration.

**The Power of Creative Machines:**

Generative AI systems, trained on vast datasets and powered by sophisticated algorithms, have demonstrated the capacity to produce art, music, text, and more that is indistinguishable from human creations. This creative prowess is not merely a technological marvel; it represents a paradigm shift in how we produce, disseminate, and interact with creative content. The potential applications span industries, from autonomous content generation in media to personalized artistic experiences for individuals. This chapter delves into the ethical dimensions that underpin the remarkable ascent of generative AI and illuminates its societal ramifications.

**The Ethical Nexus:**

At the heart of the generative AI revolution lies an intricate ethical nexus. The creative content generated by these systems prompts profound questions about authorship, ownership, attribution, and artistic integrity. Moreover, the data-driven nature of AI training can inadvertently perpetuate biases present in the data, potentially leading to the creation of discriminatory content. Balancing the remarkable creative capabilities of AI with ethical considerations is an endeavor of paramount importance. It requires navigating the uncharted waters of privacy concerns, fairness in content generation, and the development of responsible AI systems that respect diverse perspectives and adhere to ethical guidelines.

**Navigating the Societal Seas:**

Beyond the ethical quandaries, the societal impact of generative AI reverberates through multiple dimensions. The automation of content creation has the potential to disrupt employment patterns in creative industries, while AI-driven content recommendation systems influence the information people consume, potentially shaping beliefs and attitudes. As generative AI gains prominence, understanding and addressing these broader societal implications become imperative. This chapter embarks on a journey to explore the profound ethical considerations and societal impact of generative AI, shedding light on the intricate interplay between technology and the human experience.

## Bias and fairness in AI-generated content

The remarkable capabilities of generative AI have brought to the forefront a complex and pressing ethical challenge: the presence of bias in AI-generated content. Bias, whether implicit or explicit, can inadvertently seep into the content produced by AI systems, from text to images, music, and beyond. Recognizing and mitigating bias in AI-generated content is not only essential for ensuring fairness and inclusivity but also for upholding ethical standards in the rapidly evolving landscape of artificial intelligence.

## Understanding Bias in AI:

Bias in AI refers to the presence of systematic and unfair discrimination in the data, algorithms, or decisions made by AI systems. This bias can manifest in various forms, including racial, gender, socioeconomic, or cultural biases. AI systems learn from data, and if the data they are trained on contains biased patterns or discriminatory content, the AI may inadvertently reproduce these biases in its output.

## The Data Dilemma:

AI models, including generative ones, rely heavily on training data. If this data contains historical biases or reflects societal prejudices, the AI system may perpetuate those biases. For example, an AI-generated text might produce gender-biased language or a facial recognition system may be less accurate for certain ethnic groups.

## The Importance of Fairness:

Ensuring fairness in AI-generated content is paramount. Fairness means that AI systems should not discriminate against any particular group or perpetuate stereotypes. It also involves addressing issues like underrepresentation and overrepresentation of certain groups in generated content.

## Mitigating Bias in AI-Generated Content:

Addressing bias in AI-generated content is a multi-faceted challenge:

**Data Cleaning:** Begin by carefully curating and cleaning the training data to remove bias and ensure a diverse and representative dataset.

**Algorithmic Fairness:** Develop AI algorithms that are designed to be fair and unbiased. This may involve modifying loss functions and incorporating fairness constraints.

**Diverse Teams:** Building AI systems with the input of diverse teams can help identify and mitigate bias more effectively.

**Regular Auditing:** Continuously audit and evaluate the AI-generated content for bias and unfairness, and be prepared to make adjustments as needed.

## Ethical Imperative:

Ensuring that AI-generated content is free from bias and promotes fairness is not just a technical challenge but an ethical imperative. It requires ongoing vigilance, transparency, and a commitment to fostering inclusivity in AI development. As generative AI continues to shape the future of content creation, addressing bias and ensuring fairness must remain at the forefront of our ethical considerations, ultimately fostering a more equitable and inclusive digital landscape.

## Addressing the potential loss of human jobs

The advent of generative AI has unleashed a wave of automation that has the potential to significantly transform various industries. While this technological advancement brings forth remarkable possibilities, it also raises concerns about potential job displacement. This chapter delves into the complex issue of addressing the potential loss of human jobs in the wake of generative AI.

## The Impact on Employment:

Generative AI, with its ability to autonomously generate content and perform tasks traditionally executed by humans, has the potential to disrupt employment patterns across various sectors. Jobs in content creation, design, and even certain aspects of customer service could be automated, potentially leading to workforce displacement.

## Reskilling and Upskilling:

One proactive approach to address this challenge is to invest in reskilling and upskilling programs. These initiatives would empower individuals to acquire new skills and transition into roles that require a higher degree of creativity, problem-solving, and human-AI collaboration. By fostering a culture of continuous learning, society can adapt to the evolving job landscape.

## Human-AI Collaboration:

Rather than seeing generative AI as a job threat, it can be viewed as a tool for augmenting human capabilities. Human-AI collaboration has the potential to enhance productivity, efficiency, and creativity. By working alongside AI systems, individuals can leverage their unique skills and creativity while allowing AI to handle repetitive or data-intensive tasks.

## Creating New Opportunities:

The automation of certain tasks through generative AI can create new opportunities. As AI handles routine work, individuals can focus on higher-value tasks that require emotional intelligence, critical thinking, and innovation. For example, in content creation, AI can assist writers and artists by generating drafts, allowing them to refine and enrich the content.

## Policy and Regulation:

Governments and organizations must also play a role in addressing the job displacement challenge. Implementing policies and regulations that promote responsible AI deployment, worker protection, and fair labor practices can help mitigate the negative impacts on employment.

## Economic Transition:

Economies need to undergo a transition that adapts to the evolving job landscape. This might involve the creation of new industries, investment in research and development, and the development of a flexible and agile labor market.

## Ethical Considerations:

In the process of addressing the potential job displacement, ethical considerations should guide decision-making. Ensuring that the adoption of generative AI respects the dignity and livelihoods of workers is paramount.

## AI as a tool for enhancing human creativity

The integration of artificial intelligence (AI) into creative processes has opened a new frontier in human innovation and artistic expression. Rather than being viewed as a replacement for human creativity, AI is increasingly recognized as a powerful tool for enhancing and augmenting the creative capabilities of individuals and teams. This chapter explores how AI serves as a catalyst for human creativity and innovation, fostering collaborative partnerships that push the boundaries of what is achievable.

## AI-Driven Inspiration:

AI excels at processing vast amounts of data, identifying patterns, and generating novel ideas. Creative professionals in various fields, from art to music and literature, can harness

AI to inspire fresh perspectives and ideas. By analyzing trends, uncovering hidden connections, and suggesting creative inputs, AI acts as a wellspring of inspiration for human creators.

## Enhancing Efficiency and Productivity:

AI's automation capabilities streamline tedious and time-consuming tasks, liberating creatives from administrative burdens. For example, content creators can employ AI-driven tools for research, data analysis, and content generation, allowing them to focus on the more imaginative and conceptual aspects of their work. This enhanced efficiency can lead to increased productivity and faster project turnaround.

## Personalization and Customization:

AI-powered recommendation systems, prevalent in platforms like Netflix and Spotify, personalize content recommendations based on user preferences. This level of personalization extends to creative domains as well. AI can assist artists, designers, and writers in tailoring their work to individual audience tastes, fostering deeper engagement and resonance.

## Collaborative Co-Creation:

AI's potential for collaboration is perhaps its most transformative aspect. Artists, musicians, and writers are increasingly working alongside AI systems to co-create content. For instance, musicians use AI to generate musical compositions, visual artists collaborate with AI to create stunning artworks, and authors employ AI to assist in generating plot ideas or character development. These collaborative efforts leverage AI's ability to generate creative input while preserving the human artist's unique vision and intent.

## Breaking Creative Boundaries:

AI challenges preconceived creative boundaries by pushing the envelope of what is possible. In art, it enables the exploration of entirely new styles and techniques. In music, it facilitates the fusion of genres and the creation of compositions that defy traditional conventions. In literature, AI-driven narratives can take readers on unpredictable and innovative journeys. AI serves as a partner in experimentation, enabling creatives to venture into uncharted territory.

## Ethical and Responsible Use:

As AI becomes increasingly integrated into creative processes, ethical considerations are paramount. Transparency, accountability, and ensuring that AI aligns with human values are essential principles. Striking the right balance between human creativity and AI assistance requires thoughtful consideration of the ethical dimensions involved.

## Regulation and guidelines for Generative AI development

The rapid evolution of generative AI has ushered in a wave of transformative possibilities across multiple domains, from art and content creation to healthcare and finance. However, the extraordinary capabilities of generative AI also raise critical ethical, legal, and societal concerns. This chapter delves into the imperative need for regulations and guidelines in the development and deployment of generative AI, with a focus on fostering responsible and ethical innovation.

## The Ethical Imperative:

Generative AI's creative potential is accompanied by ethical complexities. AI-generated content, if not carefully regulated, may perpetuate biases, infringe on privacy, or raise issues related to intellectual property. It is essential to establish a strong ethical foundation to guide AI developers and users in the responsible use of this technology.

## Transparency and Accountability:

Regulations must emphasize transparency and accountability throughout the AI development lifecycle. Developers should document their processes, data sources, and algorithms to ensure the traceability of AI-generated content. This transparency is crucial for identifying and rectifying potential issues, including bias and fairness concerns.

## Data Privacy and Security:

Generative AI often relies on vast datasets, which can contain sensitive information. Regulations should address data privacy and security concerns, ensuring that AI systems handle data responsibly and protect individual privacy rights. Compliance with data protection laws such as GDPR and HIPAA is essential.

**Fairness and Bias Mitigation:**

Bias in AI-generated content is a significant concern. Regulations should encourage developers to proactively identify and mitigate bias in their models and datasets. AI should not perpetuate stereotypes or discriminate against any group. Fairness should be a guiding principle.

**Intellectual Property and Ownership:**

Regulations should clarify issues related to intellectual property and ownership of AI-generated content. This includes defining who owns the rights to content produced by AI systems and how attribution should be handled. Legal frameworks must adapt to the unique challenges posed by AI-generated works.

**Consumer Protection:**

Generative AI applications that interact with consumers, such as chatbots and content recommendation systems, should adhere to consumer protection regulations. Users should be informed when they are interacting with AI systems, and their rights and expectations should be protected.

**International Cooperation:**

Given the global nature of AI development and deployment, international cooperation is crucial. Harmonizing regulations and guidelines across countries can create a consistent framework for ethical AI development and reduce the risk of regulatory arbitrage.

**Innovation and Research:**

Regulations should strike a balance between fostering innovation and safeguarding ethical principles. They should encourage research and development in generative AI while setting clear boundaries for responsible use.

**Compliance and Auditing:**

Regulations should include mechanisms for compliance monitoring and auditing. Independent audits can help ensure that AI developers adhere to ethical guidelines and legal requirements.

**Education and Awareness:**

Creating guidelines and regulations is not sufficient; education and awareness efforts are necessary to inform AI developers, users, and the general public about their rights and responsibilities in the AI landscape.

# CONCLUSION

In the journey through the chapters of this book, we've explored the intricate landscape of generative AI, a realm where machines transcend mere computation to become creative collaborators with humanity. From the foundations of generative AI to its real-world applications in art, music, and text, we've witnessed the transformative power of AI to inspire, augment, and innovate. However, as with any monumental advancement, generative AI brings with it profound ethical considerations, societal impact, and regulatory challenges. In this conclusion, we reflect on the remarkable journey we've undertaken and look to the path ahead.

**Empowering Human Creativity:**

Generative AI is not merely a tool but a creative force that empowers individuals and industries to push the boundaries of human imagination. It has sparked new forms of artistry, allowed musicians to compose symphonies with machines, and aided writers in crafting narratives that challenge convention. The collaborative potential between humans and AI is boundless, with the machine serving as a muse, a co-creator, and a catalyst for human ingenuity.

**Ethical Responsibility:**

Our exploration has underscored the importance of ethical considerations in the development and deployment of generative AI. Bias and fairness, privacy concerns, and the potential for job displacement require our vigilant attention. Ethical guidelines, transparency, and accountability are essential to ensure that generative AI aligns with human values, respects individual rights, and promotes inclusivity.

**Societal Impact:**

Generative AI has the potential to reshape entire industries and alter the fabric of our daily lives. Content generation, entertainment, healthcare, and more stand to benefit from AI-driven innovation. Yet, it also poses challenges in terms of employment patterns, data privacy, and the impact on human creativity. Addressing these challenges requires a proactive, collaborative, and forward-thinking approach.

**Regulation and Guidelines:**

The need for regulation and guidelines in the development of generative AI is clear. These measures should balance innovation with responsibility, providing a framework for ethical use, data protection, intellectual property rights, and more. International cooperation is paramount, as AI transcends borders and demands a cohesive global approach.

## The Ongoing Journey:

As we conclude this exploration of generative AI, it's essential to recognize that our journey is far from over. The future holds promise and uncertainty in equal measure. The evolution of AI will continue to shape the creative landscape, human employment, and societal dynamics. Our responsibility as stewards of this technology is to navigate these waters with wisdom, compassion, and a deep commitment to fostering the creative potential of AI while safeguarding our ethical and societal values.

Generative AI is a testament to human innovation, curiosity, and the timeless quest to explore new horizons. It is a canvas upon which we paint our aspirations, a stage where human creativity takes center stage, enriched by the harmonious interplay with machines. The chapters of this book represent but a snapshot in time, a record of our collective journey into the world of generative AI. The story continues, and the possibilities are as limitless as the human imagination itself.

## Reflecting on the journey of Generative AI

As we reflect on the journey through the expansive landscape of generative AI, we find ourselves at a crossroads of immense significance. This journey, which began with the foundational principles of machine learning and creativity, has evolved into a remarkable exploration of how artificial intelligence, in its generative form, collaborates with humans to push the boundaries of imagination and innovation. Let us pause and ponder the key milestones and insights gained along this transformative path.

## The Foundations of Generative AI:

Our journey commenced with the foundational understanding of machine learning, neural networks, and the mechanisms that underpin the generative AI models of today. We explored the distinctions between supervised, unsupervised, and reinforcement learning, recognizing how these techniques provide the scaffolding for creative AI.

## The Genesis of Creativity:

Generative AI, we discovered, has unlocked the potential for creativity in machines. It birthed a new era in which algorithms compose symphonies, paint masterpieces, and craft stories with human-like finesse. This creative alchemy, rooted in the principles of autoencoders, variational autoencoders, and generative adversarial networks (GANs), has transcended the boundaries of what was once thought possible.

## Real-World Impact:

The impact of generative AI extends far beyond the confines of academia and research laboratories. We delved into the real-world applications, witnessing AI's ability to generate lifelike images, compose poetic verses, and even engage in human-like conversation. The technology has the potential to revolutionize content creation, medical diagnostics, and numerous other fields, amplifying human capabilities.

## Ethical Considerations:

Our journey highlighted the ethical considerations and challenges intertwined with generative AI. Bias and fairness, data privacy, job displacement, and intellectual property concerns demand our unwavering attention. These ethical quandaries underscore the imperative of responsible AI development and deployment.

## Human-AI Collaboration:

Perhaps one of the most profound revelations of this journey has been the symbiotic partnership between humans and AI. Rather than supplanting human creativity, generative AI acts as a muse and co-creator, augmenting our abilities and inspiring new forms of expression. This collaboration heralds a future where humans and machines collaborate harmoniously in the creative process.

## Regulation and Responsibility:

Our reflection draws us to the realization that the creative potential of generative AI must be balanced with ethical responsibility. Regulatory frameworks and guidelines are imperative to ensure that AI aligns with human values and societal norms. Striking this balance is paramount as AI becomes increasingly integrated into our lives.

## The Unfinished Odyssey:

As we conclude this reflection on the journey of generative AI, it's essential to recognize that our odyssey is far from finished. The road ahead is filled with both promise and challenges. The creative landscape will continue to evolve, driven by human ingenuity and AI's capacity to inspire and innovate.

Generative AI is a testament to the enduring human spirit of exploration and innovation. It is a testament to our ability to create tools that extend our capabilities and enrich our creative endeavors. The chapters of this journey are markers in time, signposts on a path that leads to new horizons. As we look to the future, let us embark with a spirit of curiosity, responsibility, and a deep appreciation for the limitless possibilities that await in the realm of generative AI.

## Envisioning a world with enhanced creativity and innovation

As we contemplate the profound journey through the realm of generative AI, we find ourselves at a juncture where we can envision a world transformed by the boundless possibilities this technology offers. This chapter invites us to peer into the future, one in which generative AI contributes significantly to enhanced creativity and innovation across diverse domains.

## The Creative Renaissance:

Imagine a world where generative AI catalyzes a creative renaissance. Artists, musicians, and writers collaborate seamlessly with AI, leveraging its ability to generate innovative ideas, refine artistic expressions, and transcend creative boundaries. AI becomes a trusted companion, providing inspiration and assistance while preserving the unique human touch in every creation.

## Human-AI Synergy:

In this utopian vision, human-AI synergy becomes the norm rather than the exception. AI systems understand our creative intent, offer suggestions, and adapt to our preferences. Musicians co-compose with AI-driven orchestras, architects design buildings that blend aesthetic and functional perfection, and scientists unlock the mysteries of the universe with AI-assisted simulations. This synergy amplifies our creative potential, enabling us to tackle complex challenges with ingenuity.


**Enhancing Education and Learning:**

Generative AI transforms education and learning into a dynamic, personalized experience. Students engage with AI tutors that adapt to their learning styles, generating custom-tailored content and challenges. Creativity is nurtured from an early age, with AI-powered tools inspiring young minds to explore their artistic and scientific passions.

**Content Evolution:**

Content creation takes on new dimensions. AI-driven authors craft captivating narratives, artists pioneer uncharted styles with AI-powered canvases, and filmmakers produce immersive stories with AI-assisted scripting and editing. The boundaries between creator and audience blur as AI tailors content to individual preferences, fostering deeper engagement.


**AI in Healthcare and Science:**

Generative AI revolutionizes healthcare and scientific discovery. Medical researchers employ AI to design bespoke treatments, while scientists harness AI-driven simulations to model complex phenomena. Drug discovery accelerates as AI generates molecular structures with unparalleled efficiency, leading to breakthroughs in treating diseases.

## Addressing Global Challenges:

In this visionary world, generative AI is harnessed to address global challenges. Climate scientists leverage AI for predictive modeling, urban planners optimize city designs, and policymakers use AI-driven insights to make informed decisions. AI becomes an indispensable tool for building a sustainable and equitable future.

## Ethical Guardianship:

Even in this utopian vision, the ethical considerations surrounding generative AI remain at the forefront. Responsible development and regulation ensure that AI aligns with human values, respects privacy, and promotes fairness. Societies adapt to the transformative impact of AI, fostering inclusivity and safeguarding against misuse.

## A Journey of Continuous Innovation:

Envisioning a world with enhanced creativity and innovation powered by generative AI is not the destination but a waypoint in a journey of continuous innovation. The future remains unwritten, shaped by our collective choices, creativity, and ethical stewardship. As we embark on this path, let our aspirations be boundless, our responsibility unwavering, and our commitment to harnessing AI's potential for the betterment of humanity resolute. In this vision, the future shines with the brilliance of human-AI collaboration, illuminating a path toward progress, discovery, and boundless creativity.

## The dynamic relationship between human imagination and machine learning

The evolution of machine learning, particularly in the form of generative AI, has fundamentally altered the creative landscape by ushering in a dynamic and transformative relationship between human imagination and artificial intelligence. This chapter explores the intricate dance between these two creative forces, a partnership that has the potential to reshape the way we think, create, and innovate.

## Human Imagination: The Spark of Creation:

At the heart of every creative endeavor lies the human imagination, an ethereal realm where ideas take shape and visions are born. Imagination is the wellspring of art, music, literature, and innovation. It is the driving force behind human creativity, pushing the boundaries of what is possible.

## Machine Learning as a Catalyst:

Machine learning, and more specifically generative AI, serves as a catalyst for human imagination. It complements our creative faculties by offering a vast repository of knowledge, patterns, and possibilities. AI processes vast datasets, identifies correlations, and generates content that can inspire and augment human creativity.

## Inspiration and Ideation:

Generative AI excels at generating ideas and concepts based on patterns it discerns from data. It can provide artists with novel concepts for paintings, musicians with unique chord progressions, and writers with intriguing plot twists. By exposing creators to a wealth of possibilities, AI serves as an ever-flowing source of inspiration.

## Refinement and Enhancement:

In addition to generating ideas, AI aids in the refinement and enhancement of creative works. Artists can use AI to perfect brush strokes, composers can fine-tune melodies, and authors can receive suggestions for improving prose. AI acts as a critical collaborator, helping creators realize their artistic visions with greater precision.

## Pushing Creative Boundaries:

The partnership between human imagination and AI pushes the boundaries of creativity. Artists experiment with new styles, musicians blend genres, and writers craft narratives that challenge conventions. AI encourages risk-taking and experimentation, emboldening creators to venture into uncharted territory.

## Democratizing Creativity:

Generative AI democratizes creativity by making artistic tools and insights more accessible. It empowers individuals with limited resources to create music, art, and literature. This inclusivity fosters a diverse creative ecosystem where voices from all walks of life can be heard.

## Ethical Considerations:

The dynamic relationship between human imagination and machine learning also presents ethical considerations. It is essential to ensure that AI-generated content aligns with ethical standards, avoids bias, respects privacy, and adheres to copyright and intellectual property rights.


## A Symbiotic Future:

As we look to the future, the partnership between human imagination and machine learning will continue to evolve. AI will become more intuitive, understanding and adapting to human creative intent seamlessly. The distinction between human and AI contributions in creative works will blur, and the line between creator and collaborator will become increasingly nuanced.

In this dynamic relationship, the fusion of human imagination and machine learning heralds a new era of creativity and innovation. It invites us to explore the uncharted territories of imagination, where the possibilities are as vast as the universe itself. As we embark on this journey, our responsibility lies in nurturing this symbiotic relationship, ensuring that AI remains a force for augmentation and inspiration, and that human creativity continues to flourish in its radiant glow.

# Appendix: Glossary of Terms

This glossary provides concise definitions of key terms and concepts related to generative AI and its various applications. Whether you're a beginner or an expert in the field, this resource will help you navigate the terminology and technical jargon often encountered in discussions about generative AI.

## 1. Generative AI:

Generative AI refers to a subset of artificial intelligence focused on creating data, content, or other outputs that resemble human-generated data. It encompasses a range of machine learning techniques designed to generate novel content.

## 2. Neural Network:

A neural network is a computational model inspired by the structure and function of the human brain. It's composed of interconnected nodes (neurons) organized into layers, used in various machine learning tasks, including generative AI.

## 3. Supervised Learning:

Supervised learning is a machine learning paradigm where an algorithm learns from labeled training data, making predictions or classifications based on input-output pairs.

## 4. Unsupervised Learning:

Unsupervised learning is a machine learning paradigm where an algorithm learns patterns and structures in data without explicit supervision or labeled output.

## 5. Reinforcement Learning:

Reinforcement learning is a machine learning paradigm where agents learn to make decisions by interacting with an environment and receiving rewards or penalties based on their actions.

## 6. Autoencoder:

An autoencoder is a type of neural network used for unsupervised learning. It aims to learn efficient representations of data by encoding it into a compressed form and then decoding it to reconstruct the original data.

## 7. Variational Autoencoder (VAE):

A VAE is a type of autoencoder that introduces probabilistic modeling to create a continuous and structured latent space. It is often used in generative tasks like image generation.

## 8. Generative Adversarial Network (GAN):

A GAN is a type of generative model that consists of two neural networks: a generator and a discriminator. They work together in a competitive manner, with the generator trying to produce realistic data and the discriminator trying to distinguish real from fake data.

## 9. Conditional GAN:

A conditional GAN is an extension of the GAN framework where both the generator and discriminator receive conditional information, allowing for the generation of data with specific characteristics.

## 10. StyleGAN:

StyleGAN is a type of GAN designed for image generation that focuses on controlling the style and appearance of generated images.

## 11. CycleGAN:

A CycleGAN is a GAN variant used for image-to-image translation tasks, where the network learns to convert images from one domain to another while maintaining their content.

## 12. Recurrent Neural Network (RNN):

An RNN is a type of neural network architecture particularly well-suited for sequential data. It has loops or connections that allow information to persist, making it suitable for tasks like natural language processing.

## 13. Long Short-Term Memory (LSTM):

LSTM is a type of RNN designed to handle the vanishing gradient problem, making it more effective at capturing long-range dependencies in sequential data.

## 14. Transformers:

Transformers are a type of neural network architecture that has gained prominence in natural language processing tasks due to their ability to handle sequential data efficiently. They employ self-attention mechanisms for context understanding.

## 15. Data Bias:

Data bias refers to the presence of systematic and unfair discrimination in training data, which can lead to biased AI model outputs.

## 16. Ethical AI:

Ethical AI refers to the development and deployment of artificial intelligence systems that adhere to ethical principles, respect human rights, and avoid harm or discrimination.

## 17. Fairness:

Fairness in AI refers to the concept that AI systems should not discriminate against any particular group or perpetuate biases, ensuring equal treatment for all.

## 18. Copyright and Ownership:

Copyright and ownership in the context of generative AI relate to the legal rights and ownership of content created by AI systems and the attribution of authorship.

## 19. Privacy:

Privacy concerns in AI pertain to the protection of personal data and the responsible handling of sensitive information in AI applications.

## 20. Intellectual Property (IP):

Intellectual property encompasses legal rights over creations of the mind, such as inventions, literary and artistic works, and symbols. In AI-generated content, questions may arise about IP rights and ownership.

## 21. Bias Mitigation:

Bias mitigation involves strategies and techniques to identify and reduce bias in AI models and data, ensuring fair and equitable outcomes.

## 22. Responsible AI:

Responsible AI refers to the ethical and accountable development and deployment of artificial intelligence systems, taking into consideration societal impact and potential risks.

## 23. Data Privacy Laws:

Data privacy laws are legal regulations that govern the collection, use, and protection of personal data, such as the General Data Protection Regulation (GDPR) in Europe.

This glossary serves as a reference guide to help you navigate the complex and evolving landscape of generative AI. It's a valuable resource for understanding the terminology and concepts that underpin the technology and its applications.

# Appendix: Additional Resources

Here is a curated list of additional resources to further your exploration and understanding of generative AI. These resources encompass a variety of formats, from books and academic papers to online courses and tools, to help you dive deeper into the field and stay updated on the latest developments.

***Books:***

- "Generative Deep Learning: Teaching Machines to Paint, Write, Compose, and Play" by David Foster

- "Deep Learning" by Ian Goodfellow, Yoshua Bengio, and Aaron Courville

- "Artificial Intelligence: A Guide to Intelligent Systems" by Michael Negnevitsky

- Online Courses:

- Coursera's "Sequence Models"

- Fast.ai's "Practical Deep Learning for Coders"

### **Research Papers and Journals:**

### **arXiv.org**

- A repository of preprints across various scientific fields, including machine learning and generative AI. A valuable resource for accessing the latest research papers.

- Journal of Machine Learning Research (JMLR)

- A peer-reviewed journal that publishes research articles related to machine learning, including generative models.

www.ingramcontent.com/pod-product-compliance
Lightning Source LLC
LaVergne TN
LVHW051529170726